Police Interrogation

A handbook for investigators

John Walkley

ISBN 0 85164 031 1

First reprint 1988

A Police Review Publication
Police Review Publishing Company
14 St Cross Street
London EC1N 8FE

Printed in Great Britain by Adlard & Son Ltd
Letchworth, Herts.

PREFACE

FOR twenty-six years I waited for someone else to write a book on the interrogation of suspects – all to no avail. This is the first British book ever on the subject and to get it I had to write it myself!

It does not purport to be the definitive text on the subject – far from it – but the principles described on these pages have been put to hundreds of police officers from all over the country, and without exception they have been welcomed as a major step forward in describing the reality of the skills required by police interrogators. Perhaps even more importantly they have been tried and tested in the most arduous of circumstances and been proven effective.

The book is based on my own experience in the interview room and upon over a year's full-time academic research. My thanks are due to scores of detectives, several psychologists, and salesmen – and even a few criminals.

I hope that police officers everywhere find it useful in their difficult, and usually thankless, search for the truth.

September 1987 John Walkley

To my wife Anne, who told me to stop talking about it and get on and write it

Contents

CHAPTER 1

Introduction

'POLICE officers receive no formal training in the art of interrogation. They are given some advice, in addition to instruction on the law, at training school and by colleagues, but by and large skills develop through experience.'

The above is an extract from the evidence of the Association of Chief Police Officers of England, Wales and Northern Ireland to the Royal Commission on Criminal Procedure in 1980. In its evidence the Association of Chief Police Officers said that interrogation skills were thought to 'develop through experience'. The experience referred to by the police chiefs preceded the Police and Criminal Evidence Act of 1984, and took place behind the closed doors of the interview room or cell. The interviews were neither monitored nor supervised, accounts of interviews (commonly differing) being given second-hand by interviewers and suspects. Training of police interrogators was virtually non-existent.

This unsatisfactory state of affairs was commented on by the Royal Commission in whose report (Philips, 1981) it was said:

> 'police training on interviewing should be developed in ways that will not only improve their interview techniques but also bring home to them the powerful psychological forces that are at play upon the subject and the dangers that are attendant upon these'.

Since that time efforts have been made to redress the situation, but it is still true to say that as at February, 1987, 99 per cent of police officers in this country have received no formal training in the art of interrogation of suspects, and not a single British book has been published on interrogation skills.

The field is, to say the least, wide open. Prior to the work of the Royal Commission on Criminal Procedure there had been no published research into interrogations conducted by the British police. In view of this dearth of data on the subject the Royal Commission had three studies carried out on its behalf by Irving and Hilgendorf (1980), Pauline Morris (1980) and by Paul Softley *et al* (1980). Since that time there has been no further published research in this country.

Morris (1980) noted that there were few psychological writings on the subject and little overlap between the four main perspectives on interrogation – police, legal, sociological and psychological. There were no published studies on interrogations in this country. She found that apart from those present during interviews, no one knew exactly what went on between police officer and suspect. Since it was Pauline Morris's job to review the literature on the subject, the lack of material left her in an invidious position.

Softley (1980) and his colleagues undertook the first observational study of police interviewing in this country. They observed the interviewing of a total of 218 suspects during the first half of 1979. They used the participant observer method at four separate police stations, the aims of their study being two-fold:

(i) to examine the operation of the Judges' Rules and administrative directions; and
(ii) to assess the contribution of questioning to the detection of crime.

They concluded that if the power of the police to question suspects were curbed, the numbers of offenders who escape conviction would tend to increase and the detection rate would tend to fall. Whilst concluding that interviewers kept close to the spirit (if not always to the letter) of the Judges'

Rules they found that 'confessions were often made because they were an easy and logical way out of a tense and uncomfortable situation'. They proposed that the rules were perhaps unrealistically strict.

Irving and Hilgendorf's brief was frankly psychological. They were first asked to prepare a critical study of the psychological literature on interrogation techniques and theory. Having done this and formed certain hypotheses they were invited to carry out an observational study at Brighton CID. The observations bore out much of what the earlier study had suggested. They, too, found out that interviewing plays a vital part in the investigation process and that the effectiveness of interviewers depends on the skilled use of certain techniques. In particular they described tactics which police officers at Brighton used to influence the suspect's decision-making process, and concluded that the Judges' Rules were unrealistic in principle.

The three reports from Morris, Softley, and Irving and Hilgendorf are still the only studies on interrogation so far published in Britain, and there are no published British manuals on interrogation. Hopefully this book represents the first step in the building of a body of United Kingdom literature on this important and sensitive subject.

Of course a 'How to do it' book on interrogation will not be enthusiastically received by all. In his research Walkley (1983) found that whilst the lack of literature and previous research on the subject surprised lay and police personnel alike, there was a considerable degree of ambivalence surrounding attitudes towards the study. Police officers expressed the view that revealing the secrets of the interview room might leave the service open to criticism and attack whilst producing no worthwhile benefits, since the interviewing of suspects (it was said) was a craft skill which could be learned only by experience and not by formal training methods.

The more liberal academic argument against the research was that anything which might be used to enhance investigators' ability to manipulate the decision-making process of suspects was morally indefensible. No doubt the appearance of this manual will stimulate both points of view.

The 'How to do it' manual is not new, however. Because of the lack of data in this country Irving and Hilgendorf resorted to the American police manuals. The four major manuals are Inbau and Reid (1967), O'Hara (1970), Royal and Schutt (1976) and Aubry and Caputo (1980). An extensive bibliography of all other known relevant works is included at the end of this book.

Inbau and Reid (1967) suggest there are two separate groups of interrogation techniques – those to be adopted when the interviewer is sure of the suspect's guilt and those to be adopted when he is unsure. This approach reflects the two major facets of a police interview with a suspect:

(i) *Inquisitorial*: Where the interviewer is unsure of the suspect's guilt or state of knowledge and is seeking information from him, both verbal and non-verbal, sufficient to indicate where the truth lies.

(ii) *Persuasive*: Having satisfied himself that the suspect is, for whatever reason, resisting his questioning, the interviewer uses persuasive tactics to overcome this resistance.

Later on we shall explore both of these aspects of interview. The inquisitorial stage is usually an integral part of any interrogation. Enquiry work, forensic and fingerprint evidence do not always, do not even usually, provide the degree of certainty of a suspect's guilt which investigators would prefer given an ideal world. All too often they are left with pointers towards a suspect's involvement in some crime, without their being any real degree of certainty about the matter.

Indeed, if guilt could be shown to be certain merely through enquiry work, then it is doubtful if interviewing would form the major part of the work of the Criminal Investigation Department which it does today. In practice, the interview is not just a device for changing the suspect's decision-making.

It is also exploratory in nature, with the interviewer seeking data which will help prove or disprove his hypothesis that the suspect is guilty.

There are two major assessments which a police interrogator makes when he is interviewing a suspect:

(i) Is the suspect telling lies or is he telling the truth?

(ii) Has the suspect reached that critical stage of the interview where he is trying to make up his mind whether to admit or deny the offence about which he is being questioned?

The basis on which the interviewer makes these two assessments is upon the evidence already obtained, information (which may or may not be 'evidence'), and verbal and non-verbal information from the suspect.

Interviewers are constantly making decisions based upon their perception of the truthfulness or otherwise of their suspects, and the correctness of their assessment has serious implications for the person being interviewed. For example, if an innocent person is wrongly assessed as a lie teller he may well be kept in custody longer than would otherwise be the case, so that protracted enquiries can be undertaken. Equally, if a guilty person is wrongly assessed as a truth teller he will not be interrogated as searchingly as he otherwise might have been and thereby his misdeeds will escape detection.

Perhaps even more powerfully, if an interviewer wrongly assesses the truth teller as a lie teller he may subject that suspect to questioning of a type which induces a false confession. Whilst instances of false confessions may not be as common as some would have us believe, there are well documented cases where they have occurred, and apart from the obvious damage they do to the suspect they also bring the police service and the legitimate practice of interrogation into disrepute.

Since to date there has been almost no training of lie-detection techniques for police interviewers, one may properly assume that police officers use merely instinctive methods. As Inbau and Reid (1967) advise 'with suspects whose guilt is doubtful or uncertain, the interrogator must "feel his way around" until he arrives at a decision of guilt or innocence'. This lack of clarity in describing lie-telling signals is both unhelpful and unnecessary, and in Chapter 3 we look at ways in which the interrogator can enhance his intuitive lie-detection skills and thus improve his chances of making a correct assessment.

In Chapter 4 we shall explore the concept of 'buy signs' and show how they can be used to identify that important stage in the interview when a suspect is seriously considering changing his mind about his defensive strategy. It will be argued that recognising this critical stage of the interview is important, because a subtle change in persuasive techniques is necessary at this point if the interviewer is to successfully negotiate the suspect from lie telling to truth telling.

The inquisitorial aspect of the interview can thus neatly be summarised under the catch-all heading of 'Reading the suspect'.

The other facet of the interview, persuasion, is also dealt with. Factors which help make any person more powerful as a persuader are discussed in Chapter 2. These are applicable not only to the interview room, but to any interaction in which the object is to influence the decision-making of others – from political debate to selling washing machines.

More specifically, in Chapter 5 we look at the actual words used by police interrogators to persuade suspects to change their minds, and for the first time ever we categorise these techniques with a view to using them in a structured fashion, rather than simply spraying them willy-nilly about the interview as can happen at present.

We look also at peripheral factors which can help in the task of making the interviewer more influential, and the suspect more susceptible to that influence, and as a sub-category we discuss the important topic of where to sit in the interview room (Chapter 6).

Simple questioning techniques are explored in Chapter 7, and these are coupled with descriptions of various approaches which may be helpful in varying circumstances.

Many people, both inside and outside the service, have strong views about the attitude of police officers to putting the suspect under stress as part of the process of interrogation, and this is looked at in detail in Chapter 8.

Finally, we accept that there are some people who to all intents and purposes are impervious to normal interviewing techniques. An attempt is made in Chapter 11 to describe these men and at least to put forward suggestions as to why they are so difficult.

A review of the skills required in the interview room has never been more important. The introduction of the Police and Criminal Evidence Act and the increased usage of contemporaneous notes has left many police interviewers with a feeling (indeed the certain knowledge) that they are fighting a losing battle. This is almost certainly a temporary setback. The introduction of tape recording of all interviews should introduce a new element of realism into the procedures surrounding interviews with suspects.

It is the firm belief of the author that apocryphal stories of tricks and even violence in the interview room have grossly distorted the actuality. All the techniques described in this volume can be defended on the grounds of fairness, even though many of them would have offended the Judges' Rules prior to the Police and Criminal Evidence Act. It is suggested that they could all be exposed to the light of day via the tape recorder and be fully accepted by the criminal courts of this country in the 1990s.

CHAPTER 2

The effective persuader

IN A high proportion of interviews with suspects the interviewing officer has a very clear idea of the extent of a suspect's implication in the offence about which he is being questioned. The degree of evidence required to satisfy the criminal courts of a defendant's guilt or innocence is rightly very high, but of course most people make decisions in relation to their business and social activities on the basis of far less stringent criteria. Even in courts of law, valid decisions are made without resorting to the same exacting standards, as any visit to the civil courts will confirm.

It is not unreasonable to expect police officers to adopt similarly more relaxed standards of proof in their assessment of the suspect's guilt or innocence, and it is not surprising that police interviewers are often rightly convinced of a suspect's guilt long before they have sufficient evidence to prove this in a criminal court. Frequently they are forced to the conclusion that a particular individual has committed a crime and that the only additional evidence likely to become available which will satisfy a court is the suspect's own confession.

The importance of the confession in everyday criminal occurrences cannot be over-emphasised, and although this book is directed at practitioners, a description of a typical semi-professional burglary may set the scene for non-police readers.

Dennis is a resident of Lewisham. He is a man of 30 years who has committed crime since the age of eight. Whilst not of outstanding intelligence, he has a quick and lively mind and a keen interest in maintaining his own standard of living, which includes much drinking and socialising and the regular purchase of consumer goods to satisfy himself and Hazel, the woman with whom he lives.

Dennis knows that just to the south of his home lies the commuter belt for the City of London. He knows that many of the people who live in this expensive (and extensive) area south of London will be out during the day – husbands at the office and wives at work or engaged in a myriad other activities. It is his practice to travel regularly to this commuter area to enter the expensive houses and steal the expensive jewellery he finds there.

Normally he makes a neat entry with no mess, makes a careful search of the premises and then leaves. If he finds nothing readily negotiable he leaves empty-handed. What he does steal is easily concealed. He prefers to select houses in the vicinity of a post box, and on leaving he quickly posts the stolen goods to himself at a box number. Alternatively he secretes the stolen property nearby to be picked up later. The whole process takes less than five minutes, since the only room he ever searches is the master bedroom.

Usually Dennis is not spotted. If the local community is particularly alert (and lucky) a resident may report seeing Dennis because some small thing he has done has aroused their suspicion. The police search the area and find Dennis a few hundred yards from the scene. He has nothing on him and because he is a careful criminal his criminal record has been blank for several years. All right, he does have a pair of gloves with him and his explanation for being in this high-class area is a little tenuous. He is also a bit vague as to how he arrived in the district.

The police do a thorough job. They detain Dennis on the flimsiest of evidence (they suspect that he has committed a criminal offence) and they visit every house in the area. Eventually they find the attacked house – rear door forced by bodily pressure and with a nearby garden implement – no chance of any forensic evidence here. Eventually they also find a stolen car about half a mile away – and it's from Lewisham! The police check with the collator at Lewisham police station who has several bits of information on Dennis – mainly implying that his method is thought to be to steal a car and visit surrounding areas with intent to break into houses.

Unsurprisingly, the police think that Dennis has stolen the car and broken into the house.

The fact of the matter is that they have not got a case and they know it. The Crown prosecuting solicitors would no more think of proceeding with the case against Dennis than they would against the Archbishop of Canterbury, and Dennis will have to go free – unless he is prepared to make some admission of guilt.

Remember that Dennis is a prolific burglar who is not usually spotted. If he is not convicted this time it is likely that it will be several months before the police get close to him again, during which time he will steadily have got on with his career in the field of burglary – hopefully not finding one day some elderly occupier in the house, since Dennis is known to be a bit violent and is very, very keen not to be identified.

It would be good to be able to report that through skilful and persuasive interviewing Dennis would eventually do the decent thing and admit his guilt. The truth of the matter is that under the present circumstances Dennis would, on the advice of his solicitor, say nothing and would certainly be away from the police station and on his way home within 36 hours, and probably long before then.

It is in this context that the importance of the persuasive aspect of the interview should be viewed.

There is much that the professional interrogator can do to make himself more powerful in persuading the suspect to take a particular course of action, ie to give truthful information about a particular topic. Later on the actual techniques used by police interviewers are described, but if the police officer is to be an effective persuader, it is helpful for him to understand certain general principles relating to the effects of social pressures on human beings. Not only will a knowledge of these principles help police interviewers to be more effective but it should also enable them to use their influence more sensitively.

It is likely that many police officers are unaware of the very powerful pressures that police procedures bring to bear upon suspects, and an examination of the ways in which psychologists say the effects of social pressures can be enhanced reveals that many police procedures, whilst not designed to make the suspect vulnerable to pressure, in practice do just that. Armed with this knowledge, interviewers are more likely to be aware of the possibility of false confessions from certain of their more impressionable suspects.

Police interviewers are by no means alone in seeking to influence people by persuasion – salesmen, politicians, managers, etc are seeking to do precisely the same thing all the time – and there is a considerable body of literature which reflects this interest.

In their report to the Royal Commission on Criminal Procedure, Irving & Hilgendorf (1980) summarised the mainstream of theory in this area.

(i) The effectiveness of a persuader in exerting social pressure on another is enhanced when there is an obvious status difference between the persuader and his subject, and the greater the relative status of the persuader the more likely he is to be effective.

Irving and Hilgendorf suggested that effective persuaders tend to be well dressed, well spoken, competent, well informed, well groomed and well mannered.

In a survey of 100 detectives from all over this country (Walkley, 1983), police interviewers were asked to describe the best interviewers they had ever worked with. They described those individuals as well dressed, articulate, well mannered, experienced and well prepared. In other words precisely those qualities identified in effective persuaders in other disciplines. It seems likely that the macho style interviewers of police fiction are less common (or less successful) in the real world of interrogation.

There are many ways in which the police interviewer can enhance his apparent status in the eyes of the suspect. For example by being shown a degree of deference by his colleagues or by being the person who can make things happen – even the simple act of ordering a cup of tea can convey the impression of status if handled properly.

Another simple method of enhancing the status of the interviewer is for him to be described by other officers (usually in his absence) as someone of importance, or by speaking of him in a deferential or respectful manner. The interviewer can be described as being very fair, or tough, or determined – whatever quality is felt would most impress the suspect. Research in the United States has shown that if a suspect is primed in this way then he is far more likely to see the principal as possessing the qualities described than if no priming had taken place.

The simplest method of conveying status is undoubtedly dress, coupled with general appearance and bearing. It hardly needs to be said that dress is usually the first clue to a person's status in most social interactions. If we see a man walking across London Bridge dressed in an old gaberdine mackintosh tied with string, carrying several carrier bags stuffed with belongings, we would be less than human if we did not accord him less status than if he were crossing the same bridge wearing a smart pin-stripe suit, bowler hat, carrying a furled umbrella and briefcase. A copy of the *Financial Times* might clinch the assessment! The same principles apply to the interview room. Whatever props the interviewer needs to demonstrate status should be utilised.

A simple demonstration of the way dress conveys status to suspects can be seen in the way suspects often respond differently to officers in plain clothes compared to their uniformed colleagues. Most officers can describe incidents in which a suspect has failed to respond to a uniformed officer and, when confronted by a plain clothes officer, has immediately adopted a more responsive attitude. Many of these instances cannot be accounted for by differences in technique since the attitude change can be instantaneous. They are readily explainable by the fact that many suspects attribute higher status to CID officers than to their uniformed colleagues.

Dress and general appearance are, then, very important when interviewing suspects and this should have certain implications for those officers who adopt a more casual/informal style of dress because of their role-playing in the course of their work, eg drug squad officers. In so far as their style of dress reduces their apparent status, it also reduces their potential effectiveness as interviewers. It is for this reason that at least one Metropolitan drug team, having undertaken raids and arrests in 'undercover' style clothing, will always change into smart clothing prior to the ensuing interviews.

In certain interviews it may well be that the interviewing officer, for some reason, may not be able to convince the suspect that he is of sufficiently high status, and it is on these occasions when it becomes necessary to introduce a further interviewer, perhaps a little older or of higher rank. It is not unheard of for certain interviewers to present themselves as officers of higher rank than their actual one for this purpose.

It is perhaps not inappropriate to allude to the effects of the Police and Criminal Evidence Act on the status of the interviewer. A major feature of the Act is the establishment of the custody officer as the person who has the responsibility for, and the control of, the prisoner. The procedures adopted when a suspect is brought to the police station for questioning (usually in custody) involve the custody officer immediately and manifestly taking control – to the detriment of the interviewer.

After all, the suspect knows only too well that what the

interviewer really wants to do is to get him on his own for as long as necessary so that he can use his persuasive ploys upon him. It is also no secret to the suspect that the last thing the interviewer wants is to have the presence of a third person in the interview – particularly in the form of a solicitor who is going to advise and encourage the suspect to say nothing.

Similarly the suspect also knows that the interviewer (often the arresting officer) would rather keep secret the presence of the suspect at the police station, at least for the time being, whilst he lays his hands on any accomplices whose names might crop up in the interview room. What happens as soon as the custody officer appears? The suspect is offered a solicitor and communication with anyone of his choice regarding his whereabouts.

What is more, the paraphernalia of the custody officer's charge room (yes, it is obviously his) give the arresting officer no real role – apart from describing to the custody officer the (sometimes rather weak) reasons for effecting the arrest.

Now it is obviously essential that all the above rights of the prisoner he preserved – they were all there before the Police and Criminal Evidence Act in any case. What has changed is the emphasis. In practice, the way in which many custody officers perform their task rubs in the fact that the interviewer has very little status in relation to the prisoner and very few cards to play. Bearing in mind the importance of maintaining the status of the interviewer as high as possible, detectives and custody officers should work together to ensure a strategy which, whilst giving the suspect all his rights, at the same time leaves the suspect with the impression that the interviewer does have considerable influence over what happens to the suspect, and that he is the most important person in the police station as far as the suspect is concerned.

(ii) In delivering social pressures to conform, the effective persuader must be credible, ie his own authority must be high and the credibility of his statements should be obvious.

There are many small but significant ways in which an interviewer can enhance his credibility. He can tell the suspect something which he knows to be true, decline to 'prove it' and then a little later on let the proof become obvious to the suspect, as if inadvertently. For example, if an accomplice is in custody unbeknown to the suspect, the interviewer can hint that the accomplice is locked up, but rather diffidently so that the suspect half thinks that the interviewer is bluffing. Then a little later it is a simple matter to show that the accomplice is indeed in the cell block.

Another way of increasing the credibility of statements is to say something which is apparently against the interest of the interviewer. For instance, many suspects expect 'flannel' from interviewers and will not be surprised to hear the interviewer trying to suggest that if they admit the offence there will be no prison sentence at the end of it. The interviewer who says to the suspect, 'I'm not going to pull any punches, Bill, I'm afraid you're going to have to go to prison for this, but . . .' and then continues to go on and discuss the advantages and disadvantages of confession and denial has definitely scored a point in the credibility stakes.

The suspect knows he is going to go to prison if he is convicted of, say, a bank robbery, or a rape, and will give credit to the interviewer for acknowledging this. The credibility of other statements made by the interviewer is thus marginally enhanced, since the suspect perceives that he is prepared to be truthful, even if it is apparently against his interests as an interviewer to do so.

Another simple way of improving the credibility of the interviewer is by having other people agree with what he says. Clearly his co-interviewer is an important source of such agreement, but if the interviewer has a plan of campaign then there is every reason for him to enlist the aid of his other colleagues who deal with the suspect. For instance, as discussed in the previous section, if he wants to present himself as a fair and truthful interviewer, then it can be of enormous assistance to him if the custody officer or jailer in charge of the suspect casually mentions, prior to the interview, that he in fact has these qualities. It is very much up to the interviewer to brief the custody officer as to exactly how he wishes to be represented to the suspect.

The credibility of the interviewer can, of course, be very easily destroyed. The suspect is, by definition, dubious about the *bona fides* of his interviewer and any hint that he is not trustworthy will make a considerable impact. In particular, if there is any sign of disagreement between one interviewer and another then their credibility can drop alarmingly.

A few words here about a famous American psychological experiment are perhaps not out of place to reinforce the points made so far. Many police interviewers are not conscious of the very powerful position they hold *vis-à-vis* the suspect – they do not appreciate the powerful, yet paradoxically fragile, influences exerted by a person in authority over a given subject.

Milgram advertised for volunteers to take part in a teaching experiment. The experiment was ostensibly designed to test the efficacy of punishment as a teaching aid. Volunteers were introduced to a teaching laboratory where they were invited to teach another volunteer on a one-to-one basis, ie one member of the pair was to be a teacher, the other a pupil. The pupil was attached to a rheostat through which the teacher could administer varying degrees of electrical shock whenever mistakes were made. The rheostat was calibrated from mild to dangerous and the whole experiment was supervised by a man in a white coat.

Unbeknown to the teacher, the 'pupil' was in fact an actor who simulated shock whenever the phoney rheostat was activated; and the experiment was not designed to test the efficacy of punishment as a teaching aid but rather how far the teacher would be prepared to go on inflicting pain if authorised by the man in the white coat.

To the amazement of the researchers a significant proportion (30 per cent) was prepared to go to the highest level of shock, even when told that the subject had a heart condition. The only prompting they required was reassurance from the supervisor with set formulae of words such as 'It is essential for the success of the experiment that you continue'.

There is ample subjective evidence that humans do respond to authority by performing acts which are contrary to their principles or interests (the holocaust comes to mind), but this experiment demonstrated the phenomenon in the laboratory. Tests showed that the people selected would not normally be agreeable to the infliction of pain for teaching purposes – indeed many were connected with caring vocations and were probably less inclined to this view than the norm.

The influence of the supervisor was powerful and yet at the same time fragile. His credibility could easily be destroyed. It was found that when a second supervisor came into the room and disagreed in some way with the first supervisor, then his ability to influence the subject fell dramatically.

Some police officers may feel that it is a big step to make from the psychological experiment briefly described above to the police interview room, but in truth it is not. The police officer in this country still maintains a relatively high degree of authority and credibility and this is especially true in the interview room, where he has considerable control over the behaviour of the suspect – for instance over where the suspect sits, whether or not he smokes, when he takes refreshment etc. It is argued that in real terms it should be expected that the authority of the police officer over the suspect must be significantly higher than that exercised by the man in the white coat over the volunteers who, after all, could have walked out at any time.

The purpose in recounting the experiment is twofold. Firstly, police officers should recognise the substantial influence they have over the suspect; by recognising it they are better able to utilise this influence and equally importantly they become aware that in certain cases, perhaps more than they had hitherto expected, their influence can be so great that they unwittingly place undue pressure on him.

Secondly, they should understand that their credibility with the suspect is exceedingly fragile and transitory. It can readily be reduced to nothing by displays of disagreement, no matter how slight, between interviewers or by actions which somehow reduce the status of the interviewer or the importance of the interview. For instance, if the jailer walks into the interview at a crucial stage and puts the prisoner's tea in front of him with a cheery flourish, or if the custody officer walks in unannounced and addresses the prisoner with information about the arrival of visitors or the like.

(iii) The impact of persuasion is enhanced by requiring active participation from the subject.

This particular psychological theory has been practised by salesmen for many years. One well known double-glazing company, for instance, advises its salesmen to say to prospective customers things like, 'How would you feel if we managed to cut your condensation down by X per cent?' or 'Can you see how that would eliminate draughts, Mr. Smith?' The object is to get customer participation in the selling process.

Similar tactics can be productive in the police interrogation room. Of course, certain questions could be counter productive. 'How would you feel if we managed to get you seven years' imprisonment for this particularly nasty rape, Mr. Smith?' is probably not to be recommended. But there is ample scope for discussion on such topics as the prospect of rehabilitation, recovery of stolen property for the benefit of all, attitude of others to the offence committed and the like.

There is a danger in encouraging the active participation of the suspect, namely that there is another well known psychological tenet that once an attitude has been openly expressed it is harder for a persuader to change that person's attitude. Translated to the interview situation, this means that if a suspect is allowed to persistently and openly tell lies about his involvement in the offence about which he is being questioned, then it will be harder for him later on to change his mind and tell the truth.

Thus, whilst it is of course essential to permit a suspect to tell his side of the story, once the investigator is satisfied that the story is false then it is advisable to curb the suspect's open denials to some extent. So, when a suspect denies an offence, the experienced interviewer can often be heard to say words similar to, 'Hold on, let me finish. Before you start denying it just listen to what I have got to say' and at the same time the interviewer is holding up his hands in a placatory and steadying fashion. These words and gestures are often repeated several times during the course of an interview, the object being to reduce the number of times a suspect can openly deny his involvement and hence make the final transition from lie telling to truth telling a little less painful for the suspect.

(iv) If a persuader is trying to manage a gross manipulation of his subject's behaviour his probability of success will be enhanced if he first puts statements to his subject with which the subject is known to agree.

Once again salesmen have not been slow to latch on to a psychological principle. They call it 'Questioning for agreement' or 'Getting the customer into "Yes" mode'.

'You do understand, don't you?'

'You do agree?'

'Is that all right Mr Customer?'

'Can you see how that would reduce heat loss Mr Customer?'

There is no doubting that, as far as the police interview is concerned, the attempt to influence the suspect's decision-making is gross. In the persuasive facet of the interview, the interviewer is trying to persuade the suspect to desist from lie telling and commence truth telling and to do so in the face of what the suspect considers are factors which are against his own best interests. It is then very helpful if non-threatening questions with which the suspect can agree are put to him during the early stages of the interview.

Some interviewers prefer to go through the suspect's formal particulars, name, address etc. Others prefer a more casual approach, asking the suspect about family and friends, particularly where the supect and interviewer are both known to each other, as is often the case with local criminals.

Yet other interviewers prefer to start on the meat of the interview straightaway, but at least ask questions to which the suspect can afford to give truthful answers, such as what he has been doing in the days preceding the date of the offence, current associates and the like. All this can be done whilst at the same time giving the impression of calm confidence necessary to indicate to the suspect that there is no point in his lying, since there is plenty of evidence etc (see Chapter 5).

If there is an area of agreement between the suspect and the interviewer (and there often is) it is useful to start the interview by discussing this common ground.

(v) Pressures to conform exercised by a dominant persuader are more likely to be effective if the subject is isolated from his peers.

Most police procedures which are adopted in relation to prisoners do tend to isolate them from other people. It is not recommended that suspects be deliberately isolated for long periods to make them more susceptible to police pressures since that would clearly be unfair and unacceptable. Nevertheless, interviewers should be aware of the principle for the following reasons:

(a) At times the interviewer can forget just how powerful he is in relation to the suspect's thought process. He can return a difficult suspect to his cell after a frustrating and negative interview and feel there is no hope in going on further. This is often not the case. *Whilst the suspect is waiting there alone in his cell the pressures of the interview are still continuing, even though this does not appear to be the case.*

Hands up all those interviewers who have gone back to their

supervisors and said they could get nowhere with the suspect and have been told to go back and have another go, only to be met by a prisoner who after a short while appears to have changed his tune. It is not just that persistence pays off (although it often does); it also reflects the certain truth that while a prisoner is in his cell the pressures and influences laid upon him by an experienced interviewer are still at work.

(b) Except in very special circumstances, it is almost never advisable to interview more than one suspect at the same time in one room. Usually this is only a problem during the initial period immediately prior to the arrest of a suspect, when he is with his family or friends, but there are occasionally unprofessional attempts at casual interviews at police stations where more than one suspect is present.

(c) It has to be said that the presence of a solicitor, even if he is not positively obstructive (which is less common now than of yore), is likely to be counter productive. Obviously the suspect will look to the solicitor for support of his own view that he should continue to deny the offence about which he is being questioned, and it would be very unusual if he did not get that support.

(d) Because police procedures do tend to isolate suspects from contact with other people, some suspects are more susceptible to social pressures than certain inexperienced interviewers might believe. Certain inadequate suspects, when subjected to custody, may be so far influenced by a dominant interviewer that they admit offences they have not committed. Any signs of 'capitulation' rather than 'conversion' should be carefully looked for, and in any case the normal good practice of corroborating all confessions should be carried out.

(vi) The effectiveness of social pressures to conform is enhanced by mild stress, including mild fear, uncertainty due to lack of information, information overload, or mild conflict.

Most suspects are subject to all of the above circumstances

during the course of a police interview, and once again it is necessary for police interviewers to appreciate the powerful position they are in as a result. There is usually no need (and it is not advocated) for police interviewers to attempt to induce mild stress states and mild fear into the suspect's mind. The circumstances surrounding normal arrest and interview procedures inevitably lead to mild stress and mild fear, and the interviewer need merely be aware that these states of mind make the suspect more amenable to interview.

Similarly most suspects, especially guilty suspects, suffer from uncertainty due to lack of information. The kind of questions preying on the mind of a guilty suspect when he is arrested and brought to the police station are: 'Just how much evidence have they got on me?', 'Have they got anyone else in custody?', 'What will happen to me if I say this or that?'

Information overload is also inevitable with longer interviews. The experienced interviewer overloads the suspect with the relative advantages and disadvantages of confession and denial, and inevitably this leads to mild conflict in the suspect's mind as he compares the interviewer's arguments with those ideas of his own which at the start of the interview were so firmly entrenched in his own mind.

Police attitudes towards stressing the suspect vary, and there is a more detailed discussion at Chapter 8. It can be emphasised here, however, that the psychologists refer to *mild* fear and *mild* stress as being factors which enhance the effectiveness of social pressures, not extreme stress or fear. Excessive stress or fear can have an entirely counter-productive effect, resulting in the suspect retreating from any further dialogue with the interviewer or, worse, he may capitulate and make a false confession just to placate the interviewer and remove the stressful factor from the interview.

(vii) The social pressures which aid the police interviewer in his task of influencing the decision-making of the suspect tend to have only a short-term impact on behaviour, and they weaken rapidly

once the suspect has been removed from the sphere of police influence.

Whilst the above information is not of much use to the interviewer, it perhaps helps to explain why so many suspects leave the police station and are quickly at a loss to explain to their friends and families what it was that made them admit offences.The persuasive considerations which seemed so powerful whilst in custody no longer seem plausible, and they give to their friends as a reason for confessing a reason that seems more feasible – possibly that they were abused in some way by the interviewing officers.

It also perhaps goes towards explaining another phenomenon. Many police supervisors will recall times when their officers have come to them with their eyes alight, saying if only the suspect can have bail he will go out, recover stolen property, shop his erstwhile associates and generally assist the police in their enquiries. Clearly the interviewers believe what the suspect is telling them. The suspect is duly bailed and nothing happens. How can they have been so mistaken in their assessment of the suspect's good intentions?

The answer may lie in the fact that the suspect actually believed what he was saying when making the promise. He did intend to go out, turn over a new leaf, recover property and inform on the group whose activities resulted in his arrest. But almost as soon as he has walked down the steps of the police station the influence of the interviewers begins to fall off his shoulders, and by the time he reaches home they have almost disappeared.

Those investigators who are successful in persuading their suspects to actually stick to their words are those who manage to retain their influence over them – they take them home, talk about the deal to the suspect's wife/family, get them involved. They sec thc suspect regularly (daily) and do all that is necessary to maintain the very tenuous influence they have over them.

CHAPTER 3

Reading the suspect – lie signs

'HE THAT has eyes to see and ears to hear may convince himself that no mortal can keep a secret. If his lips are silent he chatters with his fingertips; betrayal oozes out of him at every pore' – FREUD.

It has been suggested that the history of interrogation probably dates back to the time when Adam asked Eve, 'Are you sure it's all right to eat the apple?' Adam was clearly not too adept at assessing Eve's propensity for lie telling and, as in so many subsequent cases, the failure to detect the lie has had unpleasant consequences for society.

There is no disputing the fact that one of the important jobs the police interrogator has to do in the interview room is assess the truth of what the suspect is saying to him. At the present time this assessment is based on evidence obtained by investigation (in so far as it corroborates or conflicts with what the suspect is saying) and the intuitive feelings of the interviewer. There are no guidelines or advice for the interviewers to follow. Many officers believe that there is no way that the natural ability which each of us has to detect untruth in others can be enhanced.

This attitude towards the training of police interviewers in an essential skill is both unhelpful and unnecessary. Instructions on lie-detection techniques are as old as recorded history. A papyrus document found some years ago gives words of advice to members of the Egyptian Emperor's Court charged with the task of investigating cases of deliberate poisoning of high ranking officials:

> 'The person who gives poison may be recognised. He does not answer questions or they are evasive answers; he speaks nonsense, rubs the great toe along the ground and shivers; his face is discoloured; he rubs the roots of the hair with his fingers and tries by every means to leave the house.'

The papyrus referred to was written circa 900 BC and all of the symptoms of lie telling referred to in it have been described by British detectives in a recent survey (Walkley, 1983). Many of them have also been described in the American police literature. Clearly there is scope for the training of British police officers in the recognition of potential lie telling indicators.

The scientific evaluation of lie/truth telling

The most well known device for differentiating between truth telling and lie telling is the polygraph (lie detector). There is much evidence that in the hands of trained operators the use of the polygraph results in a degree of accuracy in assessing the truthfulness of suspects to the order of almost 90 per cent. Whilst there are no plans to introduce the polygraph into police interview rooms in this country, there is no reason why we should not use the principles upon which it is based to refine our current lie-detection practices.

How then does the polygraph work? In most people the act of lie telling is a stressful activity and this stress generates certain physiological responses. The polygraph monitors the blood pressure, pulse rate, respiration and galvanic skin reaction, and records the changes electronically. The polygraph examiner notes these physiological changes and uses them to assess the truthfulness of a subject.

It is recognised that there are several factors other than lie telling which can trigger these physiological responses. For example physical illness, drug and alcohol abuse, or mental disorders. An interview at a police station is in itself a stress situation for many suspects, whether innocent or guilty, and this also has to be taken into account by polygraph operators. The degree of discrimination which these polygraph examiners achieve can be measured by their success rate.

In a recent survey of 100 British detectives from all over the country the officers were invited to give examples of stress signs which they had noticed suspects exhibit during the course of interview. Unsurprisingly the physiological symptoms detected by the polygraph featured high on the list of responses. Here is a sample of the symptoms described:

Sweating (often first noticed on the upper lip or brow)
Dry mouth
Licking lips
Breath becomes stale
Yawning
Complexion changes (equally pallor and flushing)
Twitching
Trembling
Facial ticks
Blinking/flickering eyelids
Requests to use the toilet
Noticeable pulse beat (heartbeat, at carotid artery or temple)
Stammering
Tremors
Flatulence
Nervous cough
Voice pitch gets higher
Change in the pupils of the eye.

Many of the symptoms which British detectives say they observe in the interview room are those actually measured by the polygraph. Bearing in mind that the polygraph measures blood pressure, pulse rate, respiration rate and skin moisture, it is not difficult to come to the conclusion that whilst the polygraph may be more sensitive, alert detectives are already noting signs of stress in the suspect in exactly the same areas as the polygraph examiners. Indeed, the physiological symptoms observed by British detectives are, in fact, more comprehensive than those monitored by the polygraph machine, including as they do facial and other twitches, voice pitch, stammering, etc.

Of course it is not suggested that every time the suspect has a dry mouth or asks to go to the toilet or goes pale at a particular juncture, that he is necessarily lying. The symptoms described above are symptoms of stress which may or may not be caused by lie telling.

It is necessary during the early stages to carefully observe the suspect and let him settle down to the rhythm of the interview. Very often you will see that at the commencement of the interview the suspect is trying to control his non-verbal signals – he will studiously look you in the eye, he may have his arms and legs crossed, possibly even gripping the back of his chair, since he instinctively knows that if he lets himself go his body will begin to betray him. Watch for a gradual relaxation, then seek to establish a norm for his behaviour. It is only then that, when he shows symptoms of stress at a particular juncture, it is truly legitimate to consider these symptoms as potential lie signs.

It is not necessary to rely merely on physiological symptoms of stress to identify it in a suspect. Other symptoms can be found in:

(1) Displacement activity.
(2) General appearance.

Displacement activity

Displacement activity is the name given to irrelevant, inappropriate and often somewhat grotesque or bizarre behaviour which many animals (including humans) use to deal with conflict or frustration. Examples of this type of activity which can be observed in the interview room are:

Fidgeting in seat
Picking lint off clothing or brushing dust off trousers
Fiddling with hands/fingers
Tying shoe laces
Touching the head (nose, ears, hair) with the hand
Foot tapping/shuffling
Leg shaking
Biting fingernails
Biting lip
Excessive smoking.

Any detectives who have reservations about whether the above are legitimate symptoms of stress should speak to their experienced uniformed colleagues in the traffic department – they can spot symptoms of stress in humans a quarter-of-a-mile away. Ask them what their victims do when they first notice a large white car with a blue light on top in their rear-view mirror. One thing they inevitably do, which the traffic officers see, is put their hand to their head and touch their ear, or they scratch their head. True or false? The reason they do it is not a suddenly itchy ear – it is the very thing we have been discussing here, ie displacement activity.

Sometimes, in observing the general appearance of the suspect, these symptoms are not quite so easy to describe – they involve the overall posture and behaviour. The well known symptom in this category is that the suspect will not look you in the eye. Watch out for the way at the start of the interview the suspect tries to manage this by over-acting – he will not take his eyes off you, even during those parts of the conversation when it would be perfectly natural for him to look away.

Later on in the interview, when he has less control, he will tend to look away when he should be looking at you; he will gaze at the ceiling or fix his gaze on some object. He is apparently not attentive, has an uneasy/tense posture. Sometimes, although there will be an increase in hand activity (ie displacement activity), you will note a decrease in the easy use of gesticulations accompanying speech – he will 'talk' less with his hands.

Do not discount fleeting facial expressions. Psychologists have found that even though a subject may lie well with his face and have good control over his facial mobility, lie signs still 'leak out' in fleeting facial expressions which, although quickly hidden, can be detected by the alert observer.

Lie telling – the actual words used

Research has shown that many people can assess lie telling in others merely from an assessment of the actual words used. In tests it has been found that observers who have had access only to the written responses of a subject can often detect lie telling with a degree of accuracy which cannot be explained by chance.

For instance in one set of lie-detector tests, it was found that those subjects who on seeing the machine said words to the effect 'Oh, it looks like an electric chair' were more likely to be potential lie tellers than truth tellers. Well, we do not have our own version of the electric chair, but it is suggested that there are certain phrases used by suspects which interviewers believe are more likely to be uttered by lie-telling suspects than truth tellers.

In the survey of 100 detectives (Walkley, 1983) the subjects were invited to give examples of lie-telling responses. Below is an attempt to categorise these responses. It is not claimed that every response indicates lie telling, and since so far as the writer is aware this is the first ever attempt at such categorisation, the list should be treated with some care. Nevertheless, the list has now been put to several hundred police interviewers and has met with a high degree of acceptance, and it is worthy of further study and development by practitioners.

Excessive assertions of truthfulness

This is the most common verbal lie sign, both here and in the United States. It consists of the suspect over-emphasising his truthfulness; he strenuously insists that he is telling the truth. There is literary support for this lie sign – people have often accused mendacious characters of 'gilding the lily' and the classic phrase 'methinks thou doth protest too much' was also an early recognition of this particular lie sign.

By far and away the most common example of this heard in police interview rooms up and down the country is 'I swear on my baby's life I have not done this thing'. Other examples are:

'I swear on my mother's grave . . .'
'I swear on the bible/a stack of bibles . . .'
'Honestly . . .'
'You can chop my right hand off if . . .'
'As true as I'm sitting here . . .'
'To tell the truth . . .'
'There's no way I could have done that . . .'
'I can't afford to do that in my position . . .'

The above are crude examples and others will, no doubt, spring to mind. The thing to look for is the over-insistence of truthfulness on the part of the suspect.

Challenges

In this category the suspect can be seen to attempt to test the confidence of the interviewer. He challenges the interviewer to prove what he asserts – challenges him to go ahead and do what he says he is going to do, or to produce evidence or a witness. He denies the offence and throws the ball back into the interviewer's court. In the experience of police interviewers this challenging type of behaviour is most often exhibited by lie-telling subjects as opposed to truth tellers. Examples in this category are:

'You say you can prove it so go ahead and prove it . . .'

> 'If you think I've done it, charge me and we'll sort it out in court . . .'
> 'Bring that witness here then, and let him say it in front of me . . .'
> 'If you can prove it, why bother talking to me, just charge me . . .'
> 'I shall sue . . .'
> 'You've only got information, not evidence . . .'

Simple avoidance

One very clear indication of lie telling in suspects is simple avoidance of a particular issue. They may do this by saying things like:

> 'I can't remember . . .'
> 'That's it, I'm not saying any more . . .'
> 'I'm saying nowt . . .'
> 'No comment . . .'

They are vague, you just cannot pin them down. Or they talk about anything except the crime. Or they will not talk at all.

At first it may seem unfair to categorise as lie tellers those who are merely exercising their right of silence, and of course we should constantly bear in mind that this is indeed the suspect's right. Nevertheless, police interviewers have a duty to attempt to establish the truth and they should not be afraid to support the view that it is usually the potential lie tellers who exercise their right to silence, not the innocent. As it is put to the Royal Commission on Criminal Procedure by Irving and Hilgendorf (1980):

> 'The innocent, in the experience of the observer, and in the experience of every officer who discussed the subject with him, do not exercise their right of silence; they talk, usually volubly.'

This is by no means a new or novel concept. The famous English jurist and reformist, Jeremy Bentham, made the same point when he said:

> 'Innocence never takes advantage of it; innocence claims the right of speaking, as guilty invokes the privilege of silence'.

Preying on the interviewer's sympathy

Suspects are commonly said to attempt to influence the interviewer's assessment of their truthfulness by recalling that they have had previous dealings with the interviewer, and/or the conduct alleged is not the sort of thing that they would indulge in. Examples of this are:

'You know me, Mr –, if I'd done it I'd admit it . . .'
'Please believe me . . .'
'I'd tell you if I'd done it . . .'
'You know I always plead guilty if I've done something . . .'
'You know me, I don't lie . . .'
'What's the point in me lying . . .'
'What more can I say . . .'
'I don't expect you to believe me but it's true . . .'
'Well, I'm not going to admit something I haven't done . . .' (This phrase is of interest as a buy sign).
'Do you want me to admit something I haven't done?' (This is also of interest as a buy sign.)
'That isn't my style . . .'
'I've never been done for anything like that before . . .'
'You know me, I wouldn't kid you . . .'
'If I was going to do something, I'd do a big job . . .'

A bland reply to a critical question

No list of responses is given for this category, since it would consist of responses such as 'I didn't do it', or 'I wasn't there', or 'not me', or 'I was with me mate' – in other words, simple words of denial which innocent and guilty alike might be expected to make. The secret of identifying these responses as potential lie-telling signals is the context in which they are given.

They are short, sometimes repetitive answers, when the question deserves a much fuller response. So, when the suspect is asked for an account of his movements he gives, say, a two-word alibi – eg 'At home' – when, of course, he could give much more detail. It is suggested that innocent interviewees attempt to give detail hoping there is some prospect of corroboration, and in any case, as has been noted earlier, innocent people tend to talk more volubly. In tests with polygraphs it has been shown that truth tellers tend to be more talkative than lie tellers, and it may be that this is what the interviewers are picking up from the simple responses.

In addition, responding to the questions of a proficient police interviewer is a fairly complex mental process which many lie-telling suspects are ill equipped to maintain. By keeping their replies simple, short, and repetitive, they more easily present a truth-telling facade.

Dismissive or adversarial talk

The final category contains examples of typical 'criminal' talk. It is the sort of stereotypical response which one would expect from a 'criminal' or someone who is not innocent. Before they are dismissed as mere stereotypes, it should be remembered that they have all been suggested by detectives who believe they are potential lie-telling signals:

'Dunno what you're talking about . . .' (This being very common.)

'You've got the wrong one this time . . .'

'You're talking a load of crap . . .'

'I've done fuck all . . .'

'Nowt to do with me . . .'

'I've not done it and I wouldn't tell you if I had . . .'

'Why pick on me. I get blamed for every job that's done

round here . . .'
'I don't have to sit here and talk to you . . .'
'That's my story and I'm sticking to it . . .'
'It's a load of rubbish . . .'

A typical little scenario

It cannot be said that there is a typical lie-telling suspect, since different personalities will have greater or lesser degrees of success in controlling their lie-telling symptoms, and will also display different combinations of symptoms. Nevertheless, an example of one lie-telling suspect is given here because it may demonstrate how young, inexperienced interviewers may be fooled by the signals they are getting from apparently confident suspects.

The interviewer is confronted by a suspect who, at the commencement of the interview, sits in front of him, arms crossed and looking firmly into his eyes. The answers come quickly and confidently in response to the questions.

Gradually the suspect appears to get more and more confident. He appears to lose interest in the interviewer – even starts yawning when critical questions are asked; he looks around the room in a disinterested fashion, studiously brushing fluff off his jeans in an off-hand manner. He may be so disinterested that he bends down, ignoring the interviewer, and starts tying up his boot laces. If he bothers to respond at all, he says things like 'Load of crap', 'Dunno what you're talking about', and the like.

An inexperienced interviewer may feel that he has lost control over the interview and has lost the attention and respect of the suspect. This would be a big mistake. What is actually happening is that the interviewer is at a crucial point in the interview and the suspect is having difficulty in managing his responses – hence the abundance of lie-telling signals which the suspect would rather not be giving.

Validity of signals described

As can be seen, it is suggested above that a perceptive interviewer can enhance his ability to detect lie telling in a suspect by closely looking for certain physiological symptoms, by observing displacement activity, through the suspect's general appearance and posture, and by listening carefully to the things he says and the context in which he says them.

The suggestion is undoubtedly open to dispute and at the present state of knowledge it is probably difficult to be too dogmatic on either side. Nevertheless there is no doubt in the writer's mind that all interviewers can enhance their lie-detection capabilities and that a study of the principles outlined above will undoubtedly assist them in this area.

There is support for many of the principles. For instance, British police interviewers are not alone in feeling that they can somehow identify lie telling by an assessment of the actual words used by the suspect. Horvath (1973) found that even naive observers could detect lie telling merely from a study of the words used by a subject with no help from extraneous sources. Irving and Hilgendorf (1980) said that it is unclear how people do this, but suggested that one reason might be because lying responses are often deceptive whilst avoiding the outright lie.

Trower, Bryant and Argyle (1978) say that latent messages are inherent in much verbal behaviour, and it is consistent with this theory that lie signals can be detected in these latent messages, whilst Wicklander and Hunter (1975) showed that auxiliary sources of verbal and non-verbal behaviour are of considerable assistance to polygraphic examiners in increasing the accuracy of their assessments.

The use of the symptoms of stress as a means of discriminating between truth tellers and lie tellers also has some support in the literature. Reid and Arthur (1953) describe lying subjects as often looking worried and nervous, having a dry mouth, and associated symptoms such as sighing and yawning, failing to maintain eye contact and being generally fidgety. Truthful subjects, on the other hand, are said to be relaxed, lighthearted and talkative.

Benussi (1914) first showed empirically a connection between lie telling and breathing rates, and Larsen (1932) refers to changes in breathing rates as being indicative of deception.

Streeter *et al* (1977) discovered that a rise in voice pitch was indicative of deception, whilst Kraut (1978) found that observers assessed lie telling in subjects using plausibility, length of hesitation, vagueness and lack of detail, shifting in posture and grooming. In a further study Horvath (1973) found that lie-telling subjects tested by means of the polygraph could be assessed with some degree of accuracy as a result of their being untalkative, having poor eye contact with the interviewer, giving evasive answers, having nervous bodily movements and having nervous facial movements.

More generally they had 'liars' appearance'. Mehrabian (1971) found that deceitful communicators assumed less immediate positions relative to their addressees, talked less, talked slower, had more speech errors and smiled more. Ekman and Friesan (1974) described non-verbal leakage as being discernible in facial expressions (both macro and micro), eye contact and significant hand and foot movements.

A comparison between the deception indicators referred to in the literature and the signs referred to in Walkley's (1983) survey of British detectives, reveals a considerable degree of identity, giving support to the view that interviewers can identify legitimate symptoms of lie telling in the practical interview situation.

Whilst evasiveness and avoidance, short answers, verbal attacks on the interviewers, physiological symptoms of stress and non-verbal leakages are all referred to in the psychological literature, there is one striking omission, namely the excessive assertions of truthfulness to which so many British detectives referred.

Whilst it is absent from the psychological literature, it is certainly present in the American police manuals. Inbau and Reid (1967) refer to it, giving examples such as 'I hope my mother drops dead if I'm lying' and 'I'll swear on a stack of bibles'. Royal and Schutt (1976) say 'about every fifth subject interviewed/interrogated by us, who is of the very emotional classification, denies by raising his right hand and in an impassioned way says, "my right to God if I have done this"' – a clear example of an excessive assertion of truthfulness.

Discussions on how to detect lies/truth and guilt or innocence in the interview room are still fairly novel in this country, and it is perhaps helpful to look also at other cultures to see if there is any corroboration for the views expressed above. With this in mind an extract from the guidance on interrogation given to the police in Victoria, Australia, is perhaps instructive:

'*Innocent or guilty?*

The interrogator might not know whether the suspect is innocent or guilty of the accusation made against him. It is helpful to remember that experience points to certain characteristics exhibited by each class.

The innocent

- May exhibit mistrust or suspicion but not resistance.
- Often supply an excessive detail concerning trivial points.
- Tend to persistently interrupt with explanations.
- Enter their defence before they are required to do so.

The guilty

- Usually exhibit resistance.
- Confine themselves to answering questions.
- Usually answer the questions and contribute nothing further.
- May refuse to make any explanation whatsoever.
- Stress the accuracy of minor details.
- Will express the desire to help you do your job.
- Take oaths on their innocence.'

It can be seen from the above that there is broad agreement between what is taught in Australia and the principles outlined in this book.

Finally a reminder of what the ancient papyrus, some 2,000 years old, said about recognising guilt:

> 'The person who gives poison may be recognised. He does not answer questions or they are evasive answers; he speaks nonsense, rubs the great toe along the ground and shivers; his face is discoloured; he rubs the roots of the hair with his fingers and tries by every means to leave the house.'

You know, it sounds remarkably similar to the advice given in the present chapter, does it not?

CHAPTER 4

Reading the suspect – buy signs

IT IS conventional wisdom amongst detectives that interviewing must have much in common with the art of salesmanship.

One aspect of selling which is an important weapon in any salesman's armoury is the concept of the buying signal or 'buy sign'. In one of the largest selling-oriented businesses in this country, salesmen are taught to look for buy signs which are said to be identifiable by:

(i) Customer's expression.
(ii) Customer's attitude.
(iii) Customer's degree of interest in the product (eg questions asked about the product, handling the product, etc).

It is suggested that probably the most critical stage of the police interview is that point when the suspect is beginning to consider whether or not there is some merit in what the interviewer has been saying to him, and is actually thinking about admitting the offence. The interviewer has almost swayed him regarding the relative advantages and disadvantages of confession and denial, but not quite. He is still not sure.

If salesmen can be trained to identify this critical stage in the proceedings, it seems reasonable that police interviewers should also be taught to look for similar signs. Many subconsciously do this. How many times do we hear interviewers say, 'You know, for a while I thought we had him – I really thought he was going to cough'. The interviewer is merely saying he saw certain buy signs, but failed to respond to them sufficiently well to close the interview with the suspect, in just the same way that many salesmen fail to close the sale.

Before describing the signals which are likely to be given by the suspect, it is perhaps as well first to look at his likely state of mind at this stage of the interview. Most suspects when first brought to the police station have a pretty clear idea of the relative advantages and disadvantages of confession and denial. They see quite plainly that confession has disadvantages; if they admit it they will probably be charged with a criminal offence and most likely will be punished for it. Confession will also bring all sorts of other unpleasant social consequences. On the other hand, if they deny the offence they may never be found out, after all the police only think they have done it, they cannot prove it, can they?

After being subjected to the tactics and strategies of a proficient police interviewer they have been brought to the conclusion that possibly the police actually can prove the offence, that there is probably no point in denying it any longer and that, indeed, there may even be some advantage for them in admitting it. At the very least they will feel better for getting it off their chest.

The balance of advantages is, then, much more equal than they first thought, but the decision to change course has yet to be made.

American police manuals describe this as a most critical stage of the interview, and stress the importance of being able to spot that this vital stage has been reached. They are vague, however, as to exactly how this is to be accomplished.

Royal and Schutt (1976) mention the concept of buy signs and give two examples:

(i) The suspect says, 'I am not saying I did this thing, but if I did what would happen to me?'

(ii) The suspect denies an allegation which has not been put to him.

The psychological findings relative to this particular point in the interview can be summarised as follows:

(a) As the difficulty of reaching a decision increases, the time taken in deciding will increase.

(b) As the point of maximum decisional conflict arises the individual will either vacillate between alternatives, freeze, or begin some sort of displacement activity.

(c) The individual may abandon the struggle to maintain autonomy and become entirely subservient.

The concept of the buy sign was put to the 100 detectives in Walkley's (1983) survey and they were asked if they had seen suspects exhibit these signs. Almost unanimously (99 per cent) they agreed that they had seen the signs. They had no difficulty in supplying examples, which can be categorised as follows:

(i) Requests for information.
(ii) Bargaining ploys.
(iii) Classic arousal symptoms.
(iv) Posture gestures.
(v) Some degree of assent.
(vi) Response uncertainty.

British detectives were thus able to give a much more comprehensive group of buy signs than could be found in the American manuals or in the psychological literature.

The detectives answering the question on buy signs had no regard for psychological theory, but in fact their replies largely correspond with the view of the psychologists.

Requests for information

Whenever a decision has to be taken, a choice made between alternatives, the individual needs information in respect of the likely consequences of different courses of action. During the course of an interview the interrogator is the main, indeed often the only, source of information to which the suspect can turn. It is not surprising, therefore, that he should seek information from him. Of course he does not need this information until such time as he actually has a decision to make – ie he does not need it at the beginning of the interview, when he has convinced himself there is only one decision and that is to deny the offence.

Examples of the way in which suspects seek information are:

> 'What sort of sentence would a bloke get for this sort of offence?'
>
> 'I'm not saying I did it, but what would happen to me if I admit it?'
>
> 'If I admitted to a thing like this I'd lose my job (wouldn't I)?'
>
> 'My wife will leave me (won't she)?'
>
> 'Does this sort of thing get reported in the local press?'
>
> 'Anyone who'd do a thing like this must be an animal (mustn't he)?'

There are any number of permutations in which the suspect will seek information. Part of the secret of the good interviewer is to have the ability to spot those occasions when the suspect is seeking information in a particularly subtle manner. For instance, as indicated above, he may make assertions which are actually opinion-seeking. He may be testing the reactions of the interviewer to the offence, and by this means testing the reactions of others.

Once it has been identified that he is seeking information about the likely consequences of confession, then the interviewer should call to mind why this seeking of information is thought to be a buy sign – namely the suspect is trying to assess the relative consequences of confession and denial. *He is thinking about admitting it.*

Bargaining ploys

This is the buy sign which probably most commonly springs

to mind. 'If I admit it can I have bail?' is the crudest and most obvious, and has been heard in interviews up and down the country for as long as any police officer can remember, and for a long time prior to that.

Bargaining is really only an extension of the request for information – it is an attempt to not only receive information but also to influence the outcome.

Of course, almost any replies to this which indicated to the suspect that he would indeed get bail if he admitted the offence would have led to a disqualification of the admission under the old Judges' Rules, and led to the charade in which detectives would reply with set formulae such as 'You know that is not up to me, Joe', whilst at the same time implying non-verbally (and truthfully) that bail would indeed be forthcoming following the admission. Irving and Hilgendorf (1980) found that no matter what the interviewer said in such circumstances the suspect read into it a tacit assurance that bail would result.

Fortunately, with the advent of PACE, this charade need no longer take place and, providing that the information is supplied in response to the question from the suspect, and providing also that the response itself is proper, then there is no objection to a truthful answer being supplied to the suspect.

One must not assume, however, that all bargains relate to bail. They may relate to having offences taken into consideration rather than being charged, being charged with a lesser offence, receiving a visit from family or friends, requests to keep information quiet, or to keep other offenders out of the frame.

The important thing to remember in relation to any of these requests is that they are in fact buy signs. *The suspect is thinking about admitting it.*

Classic arousal symptoms

It should not be forgotten that at this stage of the interview the suspect is beginning to reach a state of mental conflict. He no longer has one simple option, and he is now wondering which alternative to choose. He is trying to make his decision on inadequate and possibly unreliable information. Alternatively he may feel he has too much conflicting information and cannot sort out the wheat from the chaff; he may be suffering from information overload.

At this point he may first decide one thing and then the other, he may try to avoid the decision completely, or he may try to find some outlet for the tensions this creates.

A simple and easily identifiable manifestation of a classic arousal symptom is when the suspect begins to cry at a certain juncture. At its most basic level, a woman shoplifter may have been confidently denying any guilty intent, but after a while tears may form in her eyes and she begins to cry. At this stage the interviewer will probably express sympathy and understanding and the suspect will then confess. It is a very simple scenario, and one which will be familiar and readily identifiable to even the novice interviewer.

Tears are not the only arousal symptom which a suspect may show, although they may be most easy to recognise as a buy sign. Frankly, most suspects are made of sterner stuff and do not burst into tears when conflict arises. Many become excited or angry, and may well demand to be put back in their cell. They may hurl abuse (and possibly the table or chairs if they are not bolted to the floor) at the interviewer.

Inexperienced interviewers could be tempted to feel they need to allow the suspect to calm down, and may return the suspect to his cell at this stage. This is exactly what the suspect wants, even though he may not realise it himself. Returning him to the cell removes the conflict for the time being, and he may well be able to retreat from the stage at which he has arrived. He may be able to resolve the conflict away from the presence of the interviewer.

It is at this point that the experienced interviewer will recognise the mental conflict and will realise that the suspect is in fact having difficulty in managing the conflict over the relative advantages and disadvantages of confession and denial. He will attempt to calm the suspect and go into the final, closing stage of the interview, using the technique described in Chapter 5.

It is not necessary to describe all the many arousal symptoms which may be exhibited as buy signs, but a description of one particularly famous one may not come amiss.

One of the very first converted terrorists in Northern Ireland was by no means a pushover for the interviewers. Since he was being held under Prevention of Terrorism legislation, it was permissible to hold him for seven days, but in the early days of the interview he refused to have any dialogue with his interviewers. He would not take a cup of tea with them, indeed he would not even accept a chair from them, preferring to lie on the floor without uttering a word. He did this for five days, with his interviewers eventually lying next to him on the floor to put their unanswered questions.

On the fifth day he got up from the floor, stood in a corner of the room, began picking his nose and flicking the pickings at his interviewers. Many lesser men might understandably have felt that they had failed to communicate, but the interviewers recognised a classic arousal symptom – the suspect could no longer manage the conflict and adopted a particularly bizarre form of displacement activity. Within two more days he had produced one of the most comprehensive lists of information on terrorist activities which had ever been elicited from a suspect.

If you see a classic arousal symptom – even one which looks particularly negative – do not ignore it. *The suspect is thinking about admitting it.*

Some degree of assent

Before finally admitting an offence, the suspect will often go some small way to agreeing with the propositions that are being put to him. Sometimes the measure of agreement is so great that it is very easily recognisable. For instance, the suspect who has always denied being anywhere near the premises at the time of the burglary who finally says, 'Well, all right, maybe I did walk past but I didn't have anything to do with going inside'. Or the indecency suspect who says, 'Well, maybe I did touch her on the thigh, but it was an accident, I just brushed against her'.

The above are two examples where there are clear indications that the suspect is going some way towards meeting the interviewer's argument. He has been persuaded, at least in part, of the value of what has been said. He has been thinking about admitting it, but is attempting to hedge his bets. They are two good examples of this type of buy sign.

Interviewers must not expect it always to be as easy as this, however; sometimes the gestures of agreement are much more subtle. The suspect may desist from denying the offence but may well not go so far as to openly agree with anything the interviewer says. He may say, 'Mmmmmm', or give some other small sign that he is just possibly prepared to give a moment's thought to what the interviewer is saying. He is no longer denying the offence, but then again he certainly is not admitting it. Sometimes he will go a little further and give a small, wry smile as if recognising the truth in something the interviewer has said.

These are first-class buy signs. The suspect is somehow acknowledging that the interviewer has a point, without saying so in so many words. He has almost reached the confession stage of the interview.

These small signs are by no means easy to detect, but they are no less valid than the more obvious ones (such as 'If I admit it can I have bail'). They are equally good indicators of the suspect's state of mind, it just takes more perception on the part of the interviewer to spot them. Recognition of such signs is partly what separates the good interviewer from the mediocre.

When this degree of assent is present *the suspect is thinking about admitting it.*

Posture gestures

Clear indications of a person's state of mind can undoubtedly be gained from studying his posture. For example, one can readily imagine the difference in posture of an alert, attentive listener and that of one not interested in the topic in hand. These differences in posture are often difficult to describe, but are no less identifiable for all that.

The most readily identifiable posture gesture in relation to buy signs is one of submission or defeat. Here the suspect may sit with his head in his hands, or his head bowed, gaze lowered. He has a defeated look on his face and has obviously come to the end of his tether. He is ready to agree to what you say.

This could be said to be the most important buy sign of all, since it may signal a potentially dangerous state of mind on the part of the suspect where he is about to abandon the struggle for autonomy and become completely subservient. Police interviewers do not want compliant, subservient suspects who are prepared to admit anything that is put to them; what is wanted is a suspect who has decided to tell the truth.

A suspect who is prepared to admit whatever is put to him on the basis that he no longer wishes to keep up the effort of disagreeing with the interviewer poses especial difficulties for the interviewer; indeed, he can be a menace. False confessions are bad enough when they are done deliberately to discredit the interview (the IRA had a deliberate policy at one time of introducing false confessions which devalued any true confessions elicited from the suspect) but when they are wrung from a defeated suspect they can do immense damage to the credibility of all other confessions and give rise to suspicions that improper methods are being used in police interview rooms.

Wherever possible (and it usually is) corroboration should be obtained of any confession, but it is never more important than in those circumstances when it is apparent that the interviewer has defeated or overwhelmed the suspect in some way.

Response uncertainty

This final buy sign is based on the principle that, as the choice between the alternatives of confession and denial becomes more difficult, the time taken to make decisions can increase considerably. In addition, in the mind of a suspect first one alternative and then the other becomes more attractive – or least unattractive. It is at this time that the suspect may vacillate between options and his response times will go up – barely perceptibly with some suspects, but with others the time can begin to run into minutes.

Sometimes the suspect can be seen almost arguing with himself – first choosing one option and then the other. With the above in mind, the following signs should be looked for:

- The suspect is silent when previously he has been talkative.
- His mind is obviously racing ahead.
- Replies get anxious.
- Replies get hesitant.
- The voice falters and he loses verbal fluency.
- The suspect sighs.
- He mumbles.
- The replies take longer.
- He uses 'delaying tactics' such as asking the interviewer to repeat things.

The importance of the buy sign

The importance of recognising the buy signs given by the suspect cannot be over emphasised. This is because it is at this stage of the interview that there must be a critical shift in the persuasive techniques used by the interviewer.

Put simply the thinking is as follows: the closer a person gets to making a decision the more persuasive are the negative consequences of that decision. So, the closer the suspect gets to making his mind up to confess, the more afraid he may become of the consequences of that confession.

In view of this, it is vital for the interviewer, once the buy sign has been exhibited, to establish what are the negative consequences of the confession as far as the suspect is concerned and then to ameliorate them. The ways in which this can be done are discussed in Chapter 5.

CHAPTER 5

Influencing the decision-making of the suspect

LORD DIPLOCK has said, 'The whole technique of skilled interrogation is to build up an atmosphere in which the initial desire to remain silent is replaced by an urge to confide in the questioner'.

There is little doubt that if this change of heart is to be achieved, the interviewer has to adopt certain measures which influence the decision-making process of the suspect.

Prior to the Police and Criminal Evidence Act the scope for such persuasion was, to say the least, limited by the Judges' Rules. It is not necessary to make a detailed examination of the Rules to see why. The spirit of the rules was encapsulated in two paragraphs:

> 'It is a fundamental condition of the admissibility in evidence against any person, equally of any oral answer given by that person to a question put by a police officer and of any statement made by that person, that it shall have been voluntary in the sense that it has not been obtained from him by fear of prejudice or hope of advantage exercised or held out by a person in authority, or by oppression.
>
> 'The principle set out in the paragraph above is overriding and applicable in all cases. Within that principle the following rules are put forward as a guide to police officers conducting investigations. Non-conformity with

these rules may render answers and statements liable to be excluded from evidence in criminal proceedings.'

In their report to the Royal Commission on Criminal Procedure, Irving and Hilgendorf (1980) said, 'Detectives are just as human as any other workers and they should not be expected to operate work systems or labour under rules which require them to be extraordinary. To do so is to invite the system to fail . . . If a person is subject to a rule he should know when he is breaking it. This cannot be said of the rules governing the conduct of interviews in respect of voluntariness and oppression.'

If the task to be performed is indeed to influence the decision-making of the suspect, then it is unrealistic to expect that a discussion of the advantages and disadvantages of confession and denial should not form part of the communication between interviewer and suspect, and yet it was precisely this that the Judges' Rules forbade. In a survey (Walkley, 1983) 100 per cent of practitioners admitted that it was not possible to successfully interview a reluctant suspect without breaking the Judges' Rules; indeed, it was an open secret between detectives and lawyers that this was the case.

With the introduction of the Police and Criminal Evidence Act the Judges' Rules no longer govern the conduct of interviews. And whilst the increased use of contemporaneous notes, the influence of the custody officer reducing the status of the interviewer, and the greater likelihood of the presence of a hostile solicitor, is making things more difficult in the interview room, it is important for interviewers to remember that at least they are no longer handicapped by the Judges' Rules themselves.

The old rules, which precluded a discussion of the advantages and disadvantages of confession and denial, are out and the following rule is in:

> *'No police officer may try to obtain answers to questions or to elicit a statement by the use of oppression, or shall indicate, except in answer to a direct question, what action*

will be taken on the part of the police if the person being interviewed answers questions, makes a statement or refuses to do either. If the person asks the officer directly what action will be taken in the event of his answering questions, making a statement or refusing to do either, then the officer may inform the person of what action the police propose to take in that event provided that that action is itself proper and warranted.'

As can be seen, there is no mention of the principle of voluntariness as previously defined. The old definition of voluntary included the phrases 'fear of prejudice or hope of advantage exercised or held out by a person in authority, or by oppression'. These have been replaced by 'the use of oppression' and the ban on informing the suspect of resultant action (except in answer to a direct question).

This means that many of the problems of yore have now gone. For instance, if the suspect now says 'If I admit it will I get bail?', the interviewer is perfectly at liberty to say 'Of course you will', providing that bail is proper and warranted. Similarly, if the question is 'What'll happen if I say no?', then the answer 'You'll be kept here whilst we make further enquiries' is also in order, again provided that this course of action is proper and warranted.

Such responses would have been more than sufficient to ensure that any confession made by the suspect would have been thrown out of court under the old rules – they are now perfectly in order.

Similarly, there is no longer anything to prevent an interviewer saying to a suspect that he will feel better if he gets it off his chest – something which was anathema only a short while ago. There is nothing to prevent the interviewer pointing out that confession is good for the suspect's family, his social life or even for the victim, since that cannot conceivably be regarded as being oppressive or relative to a course of action to be taken by the police.

All detectives reading this will have been trained that even phrases as mild as the following would render a confession inadmissible:

'You had better tell the truth.'

'I think it would be better if you made a statement and told me exactly what happened.'

'You had better tell all you know.'

'I should be obliged if you would tell us all you know about it; if you will not, of course, we can't do anything.'

'You had better split and not cover for all of them.'

'It will be best for you if you tell me how it was transacted.'

'It might be better for you to tell the truth and not a lie.'

As one detective training school put it, 'If anything is said to indicate it would be better or worse if the accused did or did not confess, then it is an improper inducement.' *This is no longer true.*

Providing there is no oppression nor (except in answer to a direct question) statements about the course of action which will result from confession or denial, then the interviewer has a free hand. What is most important now is that when a suspect confesses as a result of interview then the interviewer must do all he can to demonstrate the *reliability* of the confession. Clearly it is wrong to elicit a confession by persuading a suspect he will feel better to get it off his chest if the confession is unreliable – the courts will quite rightly disregard such confessions.

It is important for police interviewers to understand that there has been a radical change in the freedom they have to put certain propositions to the suspect before continuing with this section, since some of the techniques and phrases referred to would have offended against the Judges' Rules.

It is suggested that all are capable of legitimate usage under the Police and Criminal Evidence Act, although some would have to be used in response to questions from the suspect.

The task facing the suspect during an interview is one of decision-making. Put baldly, he has to decide whether to admit the offence or to deny it; whether to tell the truth or to lie. Many factors affect this decision-making process, not least that of whether or not he has committed the offence about which he is being questioned.

The interviewer has two major tasks: he has to assess the truthfulness or otherwise of the suspect and, if his assessment is that the suspect is telling lies, he has to try to persuade him to tell the truth.

We have already discussed how the interviewer might assess the truthfulness of the suspect. How can he influence his decision-making?

When making decisions, humans like to weigh up the consequences of one course of action compared with the consequences of another, and base their decision on the respective merits and disadvantages of each. Easy decisions are those where the consequences of one course of action are all bad, whilst the consequences of an alternative course of action are all good.

Usually, of course, life is not so simple and there are advantages and disadvantages attached to each. If advantages are thought of as plus points and disadvantages as minus points, it is possible to envisage a simple graph which will demonstrate the process. Thus, when suspects are first brought to the police station they often have a very clear idea of the advantages of denying the offence and the disadvantages of admitting it. This leaves denial well up on the plus side of the graph, with confession well down on the minus side.

It is the interviewer's task to bring the two closer together and, if possible, change the suspect's perception of the balance of advantages and disadvantages. The question is, how can he best do this?

Walkley's (1983) research indicated that detectives in this country set about the task in a very simple way by attempting to do four things:

(i) They reduce the apparent advantages of denial.

(ii) They show that the act of denial has certain penalties.

(iii) They point out that confession may have its benefits.
(iv) They let the suspect see that the disadvantages attached to confession are not so great as they at first thought.

So much for the theory. How does each tactic work in practice? The easiest way to understand is by looking at a few examples of each tactic. All police interviewers will recognise the phrases, but it is most important to understand that they fall into four discrete categories and to be able to recognise the difference between each. This is not always as easy as it might sound.

Reducing the apparent advantages of denial

The most common method used by detectives to reduce the value of the denial in the eyes of the suspect is to try to demonstrate to him that the denial is in fact worthless; it has no plus points for him, because of the weight of evidence against him:

> 'It's pointless for you to deny it, because we have evidence which puts you right in the frame.'
>
> 'You don't think we've drawn your name out of a hat, do you?'
>
> 'You wouldn't be here if we weren't sure, Joe.'
>
> 'Go ahead, deny it. You're going to be charged whether you deny it or not.'
>
> 'Your mate has made a full statement.'

The examples of this particular technique are too numerous to list. The above are crudely put to demonstrate the principle, but often what is said is much more subtle. Hints are dropped that a witness may have been out and about at the time the offence was committed; it is suggested that the accomplice is unreliable and will (has) let the suspect down; that there is evidence which cannot yet be revealed; that there is a large team of men out investigating and it is only a matter of time before they return with the vital clue.

Files of 'evidence' are examined extensively to check to see if the suspect is lying, knowing glances are exchanged between interviewers, indicating that they have access to information not communicated to the suspect, or to indicate disbelief in what he says. It is put to the suspect that he is of pretty distinctive appearance (they always seem to agree that they are) and the significance of this (ie that they have probably been seen and identified) is left hanging in the air.

It is also suggested to the suspect that there is no point in his lying because he is an inept liar, or indeed an inept criminal:

> 'There's no point in your sitting there telling lies, Joe. We can see right through you – look at you, you're trembling like a leaf – a child could see you're not telling the truth.'
>
> 'Why don't you give up crime, Joe. You always make such a mess of it, and it always ends up like this, doesn't it?'

All of the above are designed to reduce the plus value of denial to the suspect. The denial is worthless because it is contradicted by more powerful evidence. It is worthless because it is not credible. It is worthless because it will not positively affect the outcome for the suspect.

Show the suspect that denial may have its penalties

Here the interviewer goes one stage further than the previous tactic. Having demonstrated that denial does not have a positive value for the suspect, he now seeks to show that it can be counter productive.

It is in this category that interviewers must be careful not to be oppressive, and also provide information about action which will follow confession or denial only in response to a direct question from the suspect.

It is very easy to think of examples in this category which offend against the Police and Criminal Evidence Act. Obviously it would be oppressive to say to a suspect, 'If you carry on telling me a load of lies my partner here is going to knock you off your chair'. Similarly it would be wrong to say to a suspect, 'If you continue to deny this offence we are going to go out and lock up your wife and keep her here until one of you coughs'.

That having been said, there are any number of points which an interviewer can legitimately make, some in response to requests from the suspect, eg:

'By denying it and pleading not guilty you're turning a small case into a big one.'

'By stretching things out you're just imposing additional strain on your family.'

'By denying it you're showing yourself to be a liar as well as a thief. No one likes liars.'

'This will mean the little girl will have to go into the witness box. What do you think people will make of that?'

'We shall have to make enquiries down at the club. It's only fair to point out that will mean a lot more people will get to know about it than at the present.'

'You say you weren't in town that day and were out with Sonia. We know she'll back you up – she'd do anything to help you and quite right too. But we're going to prove this one against you, Joe, because of the forensic/fingerprints/witnesses/all the evidence/your mates grassing you up etc etc, and all that you'll have achieved is involving Sonia as an accessory. Is that what you want?'

'We shall have to make enquiries to check up on what you say. That will take time; in the meantime you will have to stay here.'

Once again the list is endless, but it is stressed that some of the above should only be given in response to direct questions from the suspect to comply with the elements of PACE.

Point out that confession has certain advantages

Hopefully the tactics described so far have reduced the value of the denial to the suspect considerably, but there is still some way to go before the gap is bridged between the relative advantages and disadvantages of confession and denial.

It is now time to work on the confession aspect of the interview. Once again there are many variations on a theme:

> 'I know it's a hard step to take to admit a thing like this but equally I know you have the strength to do it.' (Confession is manly!)
>
> 'Just now you feel you've reached the end of your tether, but once you've got it off your chest you're going to feel a lot better.' (Confession is good for you!)
>
> 'If you admit it and plead guilty, chances are it'll all be over and done with very quickly.'
>
> 'If you tell us where the property is, the old lady you stole it from will be grateful, and you won't be ordered to pay compensation when it gets to court.'
>
> 'Once you've admitted it, you'll be able to put all this lot behind you and turn over a new leaf.'
>
> 'You'll be able to give your side of the story.'

Once again the permutations are almost limitless – confession is good for the soul, it is good for others (family, friends, even the victim), it is purging, it represents an opportunity to change lifestyle, to get medical help, to freedom from worry, to freedom from the cells.

The consequences of confession are not as bad as the suspect fears

Examples of this tactic are just as numerous as the others, but for some reason the detectives in Walkley's (1983) survey had more difficulty in providing examples of it. Similarly in an observational study at Lincoln police station (Walkley, 1983) interviewers failed to demonstrate much proficiency in this particular technique.

It is perhaps easier to think of examples if one looks upon it as an effort to play down the seriousness of the offence, minimise the potential consequences to the suspect and to others, and to make light of any social stigma attached to the type of behaviour involved.

> 'You'd be surprised how many people do this sort of thing.'
>
> 'It's not the Crown Jewels you know.'
>
> 'I know you're on a suspended sentence and you're worried it might be implemented, but that was for theft, not this type of thing.'
>
> 'The law says the courts have to have a very good reason to send a first offender to prison, and in your case there is no such reason.'
>
> 'Of course your wife will forgive you.'
>
> 'We won't tell anyone you shopped them.'
>
> 'You're already charged with two offences, you can have this one t.i.c.'
>
> 'Once we've heard your side of the story it may not even have to go to court.'
>
> 'It looks as if it was six of one and half a dozen of the other.'
>
> 'We think that perhaps she encouraged you.'
>
> 'You're not a criminal but you do need help.'

A particularly powerful tactic in this category is to suggest to the suspect a reason for his having committed the offence which is more acceptable than his actual or probable motive:

> 'We can understand how his racist comments incensed you and caused you to lose your temper, then seeing his wallet lying there . . .'
>
> 'She laughed at you, didn't she?'
>
> 'You've got a family to support and, thanks to the way things are today, no job.'

Another way of reducing the apparent serious nature of the act committed by the suspect is to ask him a question which is designed to show that the thing you are asking him to admit to is only a degree or so more serious than something he is perfectly prepared to agree with.

There is a well known apocryphal story which is sometimes used to illustrate this particular ploy. A billionaire owner of a fleet of oil tankers met a beautiful model who had been working on location at an exclusive hotel in Park Lane. Having been introduced, the tycoon invited the model to dinner in the elegant restaurant at the hotel. They wined and dined and after the meal the billionaire, who was obviously infatuated, said, 'I have never ever done this before, but I must confess I have become so besotted with you I feel I must sleep with you. I am a very wealthy man, and am prepared to give you one million pounds for just one night of pleasure.'

The young model thought for a while, and imagined what she could do with the million pounds. 'Very well', she said, 'I agree.'

The pair had coffee and just before leaving the table the man said, 'You know, I've been thinking about my offer, and I feel I've allowed my heart to rule my head here. Will you go to bed with me for five pounds?'

'Certainly not!' she said. 'What sort of girl do you think I am?'

'We've already established what you are', said the tycoon. 'Now we're just haggling about the price.'

It is a cruel little story, but one which demonstrates the point that most people have compromised on a principle of some sort. So, the person who is insisting that he is an honest person beyond reproach and therefore refuses to allow probing questions, can be asked:

> 'Have you ever stolen anything?' – 'No.'
>
> 'Not anything ever?' – 'Certainly not.'
>
> 'Didn't you even take anything which didn't belong to you at school?' – No reply.
>
> 'Not even a pen from the office?'

Once it has been established that we are all subject to human frailty, the 'honest' suspect is on less firm ground that he should be above suspicion and beyond reproach. He has accepted that there is some degree of wrongdoing in all of us, and the interviewer has a legitimate right to question in that area.

This style of question or assertion can also be used in more serious cases – for instance the man being questioned on the murder of a young girl may (indeed he will) assert that he would never do such a thing. It is a powerful area of questioning which shows that he has committed offences lesser only in degree – eg unlawful sexual intercourse or assault.

Allied to this type of tactic one can prevent the suspect seeing the offence as blameworthy as it actually is by blaming others. Blame the victim ('The way shops set their stuff out nowadays, it's an invitation to take it'), blame society, blame the government – in fact blame anyone but the suspect.

Similarly it is as well to avoid using evocative words which draw to the suspect's attention the 'wrongness' of what he has done. Thus, it is as well to avoid the use of the word theft or steal – ask him if he took it, not if he stole it. Putting it to a suspect that he raped a victim would fall into the same category – far better to avoid the word rape and use some more innocuous substitute.

An extension of this technique involves avoiding asking the subject whether he has committed a particular offence and instead asking him why he committed it. For example, when a suspect has been exhibiting buy signs, perhaps by lengthy pauses whilst he is thinking how to answer the interviewer's questions, the interviewer might say to him quietly, 'What made you do it, Joe?'

This is a particularly powerful closing tactic since it has the three-fold advantage of:

(i) Showing confidence on the part of the interviewer. The technique implies there is no need for any further discussion of the facts because the interviewer is already aware of them.

(ii) Giving a suspect an opportunity of providing a reason for his behaviour and thereby playing down his guilt.

(iii) Allowing the suspect to avoid coming out with the hard words, 'I did it', and giving him the chance to jump to the next stage (which is much less threatening) of explaining his conduct.

As indicated above, detectives do seem to find this particular technique of reducing the apparent negative consequences of confession the most difficult to employ, and whilst all of the techniques are important this one is especially so since it must be adopted at a singularly critical point in the interview. To fully appreciate this it is necessary to recap on what was said about buy signs in the chapter on 'Reading the suspect'.

It will be recalled that buy signs indicate that the suspect has reached that stage of the interview when the balance of advantages and disadvantages of confession and denial are more or less equal, and he is seriously considering admitting the offence about which he is being questioned.

Psychologists have established that at this point of maximum conflict, at this delicate moment, at this time when the decision-making process is most finely balanced, the suspect is particularly susceptible to the potential negative consequences of one decision or the other. Put simply, the closer the suspect gets to deciding to admit an offence, the more likely it is that he will be afraid to admit it because of the apparent bad consequences of confession. The closer to confession, the stronger the negative influences.

The sort of bad consequences he may advert to are that he might go to prison, that people will despise him for what he has done, that he may be knee-capped or beaten up by his accomplices etc. It is at this point (ie once the buy sign has been exhibited) that it is important to use the final tactical ploy of minimising, or taking the suspect's mind off, the prejudical aspects of confession, and of avoiding threatening or disparaging remarks, looks, or gestures.

There are times when it is necessary for the interviewer to let the suspect know that he has done wrong in the eyes of society and that he should be ashamed of himself, but this is certainly not one of them. Nor is it the time to repeat over and over again that it is high time the suspect admitted it, that the police have plenty of evidence, that he has been shopped, left fingerprints etc, and that he will be locked up if he does not admit it.

Such tactics are especially counter productive at this time and should be avoided at all costs. It is a mistake which would usually be made only by inexperienced interviewers, since in the survey of detectives made by Walkley (1983) only 4 per cent of experienced interviewers said they would emphasise the negative consequences of denial at this time, compared with 25 per cent of inexperienced interviewers.

The questioner should remember that once a buy sign has been exhibited, the suspect is already thinking about admitting the offence about which he is being questioned. He is in the confession stage of the interview and it is the confession upon which the interviewer should be concentrating.

CHAPTER 6

Where to sit

A KEY aspect of creating a favourable environment is deciding where the protagonists in the interview are to sit. The importance in establishing the correct environment, and especially the relative positions of all the parties within that environment, should not be underestimated. In that consummate example of a battle of minds, chess, when grand masters meet days can be spent discussing and agreeing the environment so that the one does not have an unfair advantage over the other. And do not make the mistake of thinking they are being unduly fussy on those occasions, many thousands of pounds and much prestige is at stake – the decision on seating can make a difference if all else is equal.

Where do you sit in your interview room when you speak to suspects?

Well, in a survey of 100 detectives, 70 per cent indicated that they sat on one side of the interview table, whilst the suspect sat on the other. A further 20 per cent said they sat diagonally to the suspect across the corner of the table, whilst only 8 per cent sat with the suspect on the same side of the table. In the observational study at Lincoln police station none of the interviewers adopted the same-side position, 82 per cent adopted the face-to-face role, and 18 per cent sat diagonally to the suspect (Walkley, 1983).

Anyone who wants to see a subjective test of this data need only walk into almost any police interview room in the country and the chances are that he will find arrangements made for two people to sit on one side of the table and one on the other. Usually the single seat is furthest away from the door. If the casual observer then waits for an interview to take place, he will see the two detectives coming along with a man who is obviously the suspect. The three will walk into the room – the detectives ushering in the suspect first.

The suspect (if he is an old hand, and he usually is) will not wait to be asked where to sit. He will walk around the table and sit in the solitary seat. Chances are that our two detectives will then sit down opposite. Am I right?

In this section it will be argued that the proportions should really be the other way round, with most interviews taking place with the key interviewer sitting next to the suspect (albeit face-to-face on the same side of the table) with the subsidiary interviewer (and note-taker) on the opposite side.

Let us agree first that there may be occasions when the interviewer should sit across the table from the suspect. For example, if a strictly formal and authoritarian interview is required then ideally the interviewer should be on the opposite side of the table. For instance in dealing with someone who the interviewer knows may wish to be over friendly, then this may be a useful way of overcoming the problem.

There may also be a case for interviewing in this style in complex fraud cases where the object of the exercise is merely to put a series of formal questions to the suspect, accompanied with a range of documents.

Similarly, if the interviewer is for some reason very lacking in confidence *vis-à-vis* a particular suspect then the table may be a useful support for him – although in those circumstances it would be better to bring in another interviewer if possible. However . . .

A warning – sitting side-by-side with your co-interviewer may damage your interview

There is an important reason why the most commonly used position of two interviewers sitting side-by-side on the opposite side of the table to the suspect should not be used. A well known double-glazing firm does all its selling to people in their own homes, and the salesman usually tries to sell to the husband and wife together, for commercial reasons. It is difficult to manage the sale to two people, and company instructions are that wherever possible the husband and wife should be encouraged to sit side-by-side together on the sofa.

A major reason for this is so that the couple cannot exchange significant eye contact together, since it is recognised by the selling organisation that the saleman may be successfully selling to the husband, but that the sale can be lost by the merest raise of any eyebrow from the wife if that can be seen by her partner.

Our two interviewers, seated together on the same side of the table, are in the same position as the hapless husband and wife. They are involved in an interaction with the suspect in which it is vital that they maintain a common policy and understanding of what each is saying, and yet they cannot exchange significant eye contact. They have lost the benefit of non-verbal communication with each other, unless you can count a kick on the shins under the table to make a point. It is argued that the ability to make easy eye contact between fellow interviewers should be an essential prerequisite for any interview situation.

Sitting on the same side of the table as your suspect is good for your interview

There are considerable benefits to be gained by the interviewers adopting the seating position of the leading interviewer sitting on the same side of the table as the suspect, and the secondary interviewer sitting on the opposite side.

(a) If you want to give yourself the best possible chance of assessing what another person is thinking, ideally you should be able to see the whole person – ie from top to toe. The reason for this is that people who are trying to conceal their thoughts and emotions appear to give away more clues as to their state of mind with their hands, legs and feet, than with their faces. Various explanations for this are put forward – eg people lie better with their faces than with the rest of the body because the face is more mobile and expressive than other parts of their body, also they tend to lie with their face because they know that others will be paying more attention to their face in their search for clues as to inner thoughts.

Conversely they are less guarded about their leg and hand movements and so are more likely to give away secrets. For those interested, Ekman and Friesan (1974) made some interesting experiments in this area.

In an observational study at Lincoln police station the author had much confirmation of the messages given out by unguarded body movements (Walkley, 1983). There was often intense leg and foot activity on the part of the suspect indicating that he was far from calm, when observation of the upper part of the body suggested that the suspect was managing to maintain control of his posture, gaze, facial expression and displacement activity.

For example, on one occasion a suspect was being interviewed about a series of thefts, and whilst he had made some admissions had not revealed whether or not he had an accomplice. He showed no signs of lack of composure except on those occasions when the interviewers broached the subject of whom he had been associating with over the previous weeks. Each time this was raised the suspect's leg began to jerk up and down, but the movement was beneath the table and out of the eye line of the interviewers. Eventually, when it was put to him forcefully that he was telling lies and that he did indeed have an accomplice, the suspect appeared to get insufficient relief from the leg movement and pushed his chair back, beating a rapid tattoo on the seat with his hands as he did so.

The interview was concluded at this point, with the interviewers being obliged to accept his tale of acting alone. The researcher then asked the two interviewers for their views of the suspect – in particular whether they had noticed any signs of stress. Both told the researcher they had felt the suspect had been particularly cool, calm and collected. They would most certainly not have formed this view had they had sight of the whole of the suspect's body.

(b) If it is accepted that an important part of the interviewing process is influencing the decision-making of the suspect, then lessons can be learned from other walks of life. If a captain of industry wants to give out instructions expecting them to be obeyed, then there is no reason why he should not just sit behind his desk and issue the orders. If, however, he wants to *influence* people, he does not invite them to his office and hector them from behind his desk. Instead he has an area in his office laid out in such a way that he can sit with them, and alongside them – and the reason for this is that his power of persuasion is the greater when he removes the barrier of the desk.

(c) At some stage in the interview, and always after the suspect has given a buy sign, the interviewer is going to have to allay some fear which the suspect may have – that if he admits it he will go to prison, it will be in the papers, no one will love him any more, he will be knee-capped – depending on the type of the offence about which he is being interviewed.

Even the terminology of 'being on the same side' indicates the importance of the lack of a barrier between the two at this critical time. It is quite commonplace for experienced interviewers to actually touch the suspect at this stage in a gesture of support and friendship. If the interviewer is on the opposite side of the table such a gesture is limited, whereas when sitting close to the suspect the whole range of gestures from a fleeting touch to an arm round the shoulder can be employed.

Interviewers in the United States are in this respect ahead of their colleagues in the UK. For many years the American manuals have advocated the removal of the table as a barrier between interviewer and suspect.

Inbau and Reid (1967) indicate that the interrogator should sit 'fairly close' to the suspect and are emphatic that there should be no obstructions (table or furniture) between the two. They consider that not only do distance and obstructions create a psychological barrier between interviewer and suspect, but also the suspect may be comforted by the protection and support offered by a table.

Royal and Schutt (1976) say that the suspect should be seated in such a way that the whole of his body action can be observed, a situation which clearly does not obtain in the seating positions which most British police officers adopt.

Aubry and Caputo (1980) go a little further. They describe the ideal interview room in some detail, even going so far as to indicate that the floor should be smooth, with the suspect's chair having rubber studs on the legs and the interviewer's brass studs. This means that the suspect's chair is relatively immobile, whilst the interviewer can make subtle, imperceptible changes of position in relation to the suspect throughout the interview. They suggest experimenting by conducting interviews where there is no table or desk at all, and in the event of their being a table in the room they suggest interviewer and suspect sit side by side.

Compare this with the British approach where much of the furniture is bolted or chained to the floor and gives little scope for experiment.

If there is to be one simple (yet major) influence which this book is to have on its readers then let it be that, having put it down, they will do what they can to change the police interview rooms so that they become more flexible and, more importantly, change old ingrained habits which encourage the suspect to sit on one side of the table and interviewers on the other.

It is fully appreciated that the changed seating arrangements will not be easy for everyone. The less confident interviewers will feel strange and somewhat naked without the table acting as a support and barrier between themselves and the suspect. Just remember, the suspect will feel very much more exposed – and there is nothing that he can do about it.

CHAPTER 7

It's the way you tell 'em

IN CHAPTER 5 we described some of the words used by police interviewers in an effort to describe the basic four persuasive factors in an interview, revolving around the advantages and disadvantages of confession and denial.

It would be a very foolish man who thought that a mere repetition of a few set phrases would be sufficient to persuade anyone that they would be well advised to admit an offence for which they were likely to get several years, or even several months, in prison.

Obviously there is a great deal more to it than that. The manner in which the questions or assertions are couched, and the overall strategy adopted, must also have a significant impact on the suspect.

Questioning techniques

A novice interviewer could be forgiven for thinking that the average interview consisted of a series of quick-fire questions barked alternately at the suspect by two hard-eyed and persistent interrogators, for such is the stuff of melodrama. The stereotype interview has the suspect bemused by this type of questioning, looking helplessly from one of his tormentors to the other.

Anyone who has tried this technique will be able to confirm that is exactly the suspect's response. He responds similarly to the single interviewer who asks a number of questions in one, since most suspects are incapable, and certainly unwilling, to carefully remember each separate question within a question and then go on to deal with each item in a logical fashion. It is difficult enough for willing and experienced handlers of such questions (eg politicians) let alone our hapless and unwilling suspect.

So often interviewers can be heard to ramble through a lengthy question – often containing double negatives:

> 'You say it's not true that you weren't with Joe that night, and yet we know different. What do you think Joe has to say about that; do you think he's backing you up on this? You were there, weren't you?'

No wonder the suspect does not reply or, if he does, only replies to the last part of the question.

The interviewer who is sloppy in his questioning technique will also have difficulty in reading the suspect. For instance, are the suspect's response times longer than they should be because he is exhibiting a 'buy sign' or are they hesitant because he is having difficulty understanding the question? Does the suspect say, 'I'm sorry, can you say that again?' to give himself time to think, or is it the result of a badly phrased question?

It is by no means easy to question in such a way that all the criteria for a successful interview are met, and in order to structure our thinking about questioning techniques it is perhaps helpful to categorise questions in the following way:

(i) Closed questions
(ii) Open questions
(iii) The voluble interrogator
(iv) Leading questions
(v) Echo questions.
(vi) Silence as a question
(vii) Reinforcement.

Closed questions

A closed question is one which clearly defines the parameters within which the subject is expected to answer, and usually specifies the anticipated content. This effectively restricts the subject to a simple factual answer and such questions are usually less intellectually taxing than open questions.

Examples of closed questions can be found in requests for specific items of information, such as personal particulars (eg name and date of birth, registration number of vehicle) but are not confined to these. Other examples are:

(a) 'How often do you take the dog for a walk, then?'
(b) 'Which pub did you use?'
(c) 'Who did you go with?'

Sometimes the questions are framed in such a way that they limit the suspect's range of options even further, by giving him the choice of only two replies:

(a) 'Did you stay in or go out?'
(b) 'Did you use a screwdriver or a crow-bar?'
(c) 'Who went with you that time, Tom or Harry?'

As can be seen from the above, closed questions are useful for directing the mind of a suspect towards a specific line of thought and for stimulating a specific response, but they are relatively easy for the suspect to answer and are not a good vehicle for probing the suspect's thinking processes or for eliciting from him non-verbal signals.

Because the responses are prompted by the interviewer, if the interviewer is on the wrong track it is easy for the suspect to keep him there. Closed questions also tend to give the suspect information about the interviewer's thinking process, since they show clearly the precise type of information required. They are also marginally more demanding on the interviewer, since responses tend to be short and sharp and, if the momentum of the interview is to be maintained, a further question following the line needs to be framed pretty quickly.

That is not to say that closed questions are of no value to the interviewer. Obviously they are useful for eliciting specific items of information, and they do make it difficult for a suspect to waffle or hedge when he is in a problematical area.

They are especially useful in the persuasive aspect of the interview. When the interviewer is attempting to indicate the various advantages and disadvantages of confession or denial, many questions need to be put to the suspect which are designed to elicit responses from him which demonstrate a particular point the interviewer wants to make. They can be signally effective when used in combination with an open question as described below.

Open questions

Open questions are probably more interesting and potentially rewarding to the interviewer than are closed questions. They are particularly useful in the investigative aspect of the interview, when the questioner is closely concerned with reading the suspect and with assessing the degree of implication (if any) he has in the crime about which he is being questioned.

They may be described as questions which invite the subject to set his own parameters within which the question may be answered. The depth in which the suspect responds rests with him, and so the interviewer can exercise his own judgement regarding the quality of response as well as the content.

Open questions are extremely versatile when compared with closed questions. They can be used to elicit facts, emotions and beliefs.

For example:

(a) 'Tell me what you did that night?' – elicits facts.

(b) 'And how did you feel when you saw him do that?' — solicits views on the individual's emotions.

(c) 'What do you think about a united Ireland?' – seeks to examine the subject's beliefs.

Questions of this nature can be incredibly testing for many suspects, and when they deal with critical aspects of the case the non-verbal indications from the suspect can be as valuable as the verbal. It is as a result of open questions that most lie signs and buy signs are exhibited, and if the interviewer conducts a narrow interview with many closed questions, he may elicit a lot of factual information but will have had little opportunity to really test the state of mind of the person being questioned.

Open questions can, of course, be combined with closed questions so that the two are complementary. For example, if the interviewer wants to suggest to a suspect that one of the disadvantages of not being completely truthful is that there may be an adverse effect on the subject's family, then a simple combination of these two types of questions might be:

Q. 'Let's see, how many children have you got Joe?' (*Closed*)

A. 'Two.'

Q. 'How old are they?' (*Closed*)

A. 'Wayne's 8 and Julie's 10.'

Q. 'And how is it going to affect them if you take all the blame for this and have to do a full stretch?' (*Open*)

As can be seen, the two closed questions pave the way for the more difficult open question and make its impact that little bit more forceful.

It is a technique which may often be used – particularly with suspects who are having genuine difficulty in answering. The series of easy questions before the difficult one maintain the momentum of the interviewer and keep the suspect in the frame of mind where he will at least attempt to answer.

The voluble interrogator

It is true to say that many interviewers do far too much talking and not enough listening. An ideal interview should consist of short, easily understood questions followed by lengthy answers which tax the thought processes of the suspect to the full. Once the interviewer learns the art of open questions they are easier to formulate than closed questions, and allow the questioner much more time to think carefully about the replies he is getting.

'How did you feel about that?'
'What was their response?'
'Tell me a little bit more about that, then?'
'What made you take that course of action?'

The above are all short questions which are easy to formulate and the responses should take considerably longer, giving the questioner plenty of listening and evaluation time. The frequent use of open questions enhances the ability of the interviewer to listen to what the suspect has to say, and this is yet another reason why this type of question must feature prominently in most successful interviews.

Leading questions

All police officers are very familiar with the concept of leading questions, having discussed them at training school in relation to their use by lawyers in the criminal courts. The leading question is merely a specialised type of closed question in which the answer is assumed or suggested in the question. For example:

'You were with Tom that night, weren't you.'

There is no objection to leading questions being used during an interrogation, but they are subject to all the problems of other types of closed question – only more so. When used, it should be because the interviewer wishes to assess the suspect's response to an assertion, or to set up the suspect for an open question as described above.

Echo questions

There is an interesting kind of question which can be used to probe deeper and deeper into a subject's thought processes. In certain emotional suspects it can generate stress responses and the interviewer should be aware of this. Nevertheless it can be very useful on occasions, particularly if the offence has been committed at an emotional level – say a violent sexual assault.

The technique consists of taking up the suspect's last response and repeating it in a question manner, causing the suspect himself to examine the response and comment further upon it.

For example:

Q. 'How did you feel when she said she didn't want you to walk her home?' (*Open*)
A. 'I suppose I was a bit annoyed.'
Q. 'So you were annoyed with the girl?' (*Echo*)
A. 'Yes, but I wouldn't have done her any harm. It was just that earlier on I thought she fancied me.'
Q. 'You thought she'd taken a fancy to you?' (*Echo*)
A. 'Yes, you know she was kissing me and like looking at me and I thought I was in.'
Q. 'So you thought you were in?' (*Echo*)
A. 'Yes, anyone would, she was acting like a dead cert.'
Q. 'She was acting like a dead cert, was she?' (*Echo*)
A. 'I'll say. For all I knew she could have been on the game. In fact I reckon she was on the game.'
Q. 'So you thought she might be a prostitute?' (*Echo*)
A. 'Wouldn't you? She had a skirt up round her arse and more paint than the Forth Bridge.'
Q. 'How do you feel about prostitutes?' (*Open*)

As indicated above, the echo question can be a useful method of attempting to probe the feelings and emotions of the suspect. Providing the echoing is done sensitively the results will not sound contrived, and because the question is in effect a repetition of something which the subject has already said he finds it difficult to refute. If he does not like what he hears he will try and explain his way out of it, and this gives further clues as to his state of mind, either because of what he reveals or because of what he attempts to conceal. It is worth repeating, however, that the technique can be a potent tool for probing the suspect's thought processes, and may prove stressful if the suspect is susceptible to the technique.

Silence

Contrary to what many interrogators appear to think, it is not absolutely essential to fill every gap in the interview with words. Whilst it is important for interviewers to be verbally fluent it is not necessary that they demonstrate this fluency at every touch and turn. During the latter part of the interview, when the suspect may be exhibiting buy signs and be taking longer to respond to questions, he should be allowed time to think through his answers unless he is ready for the interviewer to take the interview into its close by using the technique of reducing the apparent negative consequences of admission.

Silence may also be used as a powerful method of eliciting a more detailed response – television interviewers do this all the time to put pressure on their unwitting interviewees. We have all witnessed the emotional subject on television who, having responded emotionally to a particular question, has then been subjected to a pregnant pause with the ensuing silence on the part of the interviewer being rewarded by the anticipated flood of tears.

Silence can be just as powerful in the interview room. It is not a technique to be used early on in the interview, but once a rapport has been built with the suspect, he will feel almost duty bound to respond to fill any lengthy silences – usually by elaborating upon an answer already given.

Reinforcement

If you want a favourable response to a question then it is obviously no good asking it in a manner which upsets the respondent; but merely asking the question in a polite or authoritative fashion is not sufficient to ensure the suspect is forthcoming in his replies. He needs encouragement, or in the jargon of the psychologists social reward or reinforcement.

Psychological experiments in which dogs and budgies ring

bells in response to rewards are so well known (Pavlov springs to mind) that they hardly need repeating, and random rewards for doing the right thing (ie sometimes you get the reward, sometimes you don't) appear to be particularly powerful – fruit machines work on this principle and a lot of entrepreneurs have become millionaires whilst punters have eagerly proved how right the psychologists are!

Just as social reward actually encourages a course of action, so lack of social reward tends to discourage. If a suspect continually receives negative feedback in response to a particular line of reply, then it will become increasingly difficult for him to persist with it.

By the judicious use of reinforcement ploys, the interviewer can exercise control over the suspect and steer him towards a particular avenue.

Police officers in the interview situation are fortunate compared to television interviewers, who also recognise the need to provide reinforcement to their interviewees. Usually television interviewers are in a position where they should not show too much bias, and yet they need to encourage their subjects to go along a particular road. As a glance at almost any such interview will show, they do it non-verbally by vigorous nodding of the head – often grossly exaggerated – and by smiling. The exaggeration is necessary because when a subject is highly stressed or aroused, the need for reinforcement is usually greater than normal – and like police suspects, television interviewees are usually subject to stress and arousal.

As indicated, reinforcement can be verbal or non-verbal and can be split into three categories:

Expressions of approval

Verbal

'That's good.'

'Yes.'

'I like that approach.'

'Fine.'
'Go on.'
Non-verbal
Nodding
Smiling
Looking at fellow interviewer as if to say, 'He's right, you know.'
Encouraging sounds other than words – eg Uh huh, Mmmm.

Expressions of support
Verbal
'I can go along with that.'
'I understand.'
'That's OK.'
'Of course.'
'I know.'
Non-verbal
Lean forward attentively
Touch in a gesture of friendship

Compliments
Verbal
'Not many people in your position would have had the guts to say that.'
'You're no fool, you know.'
'You're quite a character.'
'You're a funny bugger, but you're straight John Bull.'
Non-verbal
Give a little shake of the head as if to indicate 'I've got to admire you for saying that.' Sit back in your chair as you are doing it.
Give a slightly longer eye contact after the response and accompany it with a faint smile.

The principle behind all of the above is to make the suspect feel good when he is responding in a certain fashion. There will probably be little call for the technique during the early stages of the interview, since the suspect will largely be replying in a negative way, but of course the very absence of reinforcement in the early stages is a useful ploy. Later, particularly after the suspect has exhibited a buy sign, any small step he makes towards telling the truth should be rewarded in some way.

When he takes the final step of admitting the offence then the rewarding process should continue – making an admission can have a cathartic effect and the suspect should be encouraged to feel good about it. The release from tension should be aided and the interviewer should foster the feeling that further revelations will bring even more benefits. If handled sensitively, it is at this time that the persistent criminal can be persuaded to admit further offences, or the terrorist be converted.

CHAPTER 8

Stratagems

IT IS not realistic to think that any one individual's personal character will be suited to the interrogation of all suspect types and in relation to all offences. For this reason it is necessary for interviewers to adopt various stratagems in the pursuit of their art.

The most well known of these stratagems is the 'hard man/ soft man' routine or, as some prefer to call it, 'Mutt and Jeff' or 'sweet and sour'. Indeed, this approach is so hackneyed that it has become the stereotype for most dramatisations of police interrogation practices.

Before attempting to categorise a few stratagems it is as well to look once again at the scenario the interviewer is trying to create.

He is trying to present himself as a person of some status *vis-à-vis* the suspect, one who has control over events affecting the suspect's own circumstances, who is credible and who is knowledgeable about the case in hand. Initially he would like the suspect to be subject to mild stress, to be apprehensive and to rely on the interviewer for information.

He knows that during the course of the interview he is going to have to convince the suspect that confession has fewer disadvantages than he at first thought, indeed that it has certain advantages. In addition he will want to demonstrate that there is little if any advantage in denial, and that there is some risk attached to it.

During the course of the interview at least one of the interviewers is going to have to form a rapport with the suspect, so that when the critical buy sign is exhibited he is in a position to convince the suspect that he has little to fear from confession.

Quite a tall order!

Stress and the suspect

Irving and Hilgendorf (1980) in their summary of the factors which enhance the effectiveness of social pressures refer to mild stress and mild fear as important considerations, and in the folklore surrounding the art of interrogation much is made of the stress under which suspects are put – the swinging light bulb and the dripping tap have become clichés. To what extent do they reflect the reality?

In a survey of 100 detectives from all over the country (Walkley, 1983) the subjects were asked the following question:

> 'If you were interviewing a man whom you suspected of a bad case of rape on a respectable teenage girl would you be prepared to put mental pressure on that suspect to make him tell the truth?'

In response, 92 per cent of the sample replied that they would be prepared to put mental pressure on the suspect in such cases. This overwhelming response is a clear indication that interviewers are prepared to put the suspect under some stress if the occasion warrants it.

In response to another question, 'Is it good or bad if you make the suspect slightly anxious?', 73 per cent responded that it was good compared with only 11 per cent who said it was bad. This compares with the responses to a similar question on whether it was good or bad to make the suspect feel really relaxed in which 46 per cent said it was good, 36 per cent said it was bad, and 14 per cent said 'it depends'.

The sample was equally split between experienced and

inexperienced interviewers and in the survey experienced interviewers had a greater tendency towards accepting that stress was potentially beneficial, and less of a tendency towards believing that relaxing the suspect was beneficial.

For example, there are at least two different ways of treating the suspect whilst in the car on the way to the police station. One can chat to him (not necessarily about the offence) or one can maintain a stony silence. Experienced interviewers were twice as likely to maintain silence as inexperienced interviewers, although a significant minority recognised that much depended on the demeanour of the suspect.

Similarly, experienced detectives were almost twice as likely to think it bad practice if the suspect were to be given plenty of reading material whilst he was waiting to be interviewed – indeed only 4 per cent thought it to be a good thing. This compares with 21 per cent of inexperienced officers who thought it would be good practice.

A significant minority (approximately 30 per cent) wrongly thought that the attitude of the jailer or custodian was not an important factor in the interview. Since the advent of the Police and Criminal Evidence Act it is unlikely that so many would still make this mistake.

The survey indicated that whilst a majority of interviewers were perfectly prepared to put stress on suspects, only a very small proportion of officers would countenance any real physical violence towards a prisoner, although most will hint at it.

What are the implications for interviewing officers?

Firstly it should never be forgotten that it is mild stress and mild fear that aid the interview. If, when a suspect is first arrested, he is obviously very frightened or intimidated it is just as important to calm his fears as it is to take control of the over-confident suspect. Thus whilst it is good practice in many cases to treat the suspect coldly on the way to the police station, if he is an extremely nervous suspect a kind word or two may help bring his stress level down a little.

Secondly the role of the officers who look after prisoners is absolutely vital. If you have a difficult prisoner who is obviously confident and very much in control of himself and his surroundings, then it could be unhelpful if the custody officer and jailer increase his comfort level unnecessarily. They should form part of your team and it is important that you and they discuss the approach which is most likely to be successful with any particular prisoner.

Whilst it is important that the provisions of the Police and Criminal Evidence Act be abided by, the degree to which the prisoner is made to feel 'at home' is entirely out of the scope of PACE, and whilst some prisoners do need coddling, it is likely that for the relatively short duration that the remainder remain in custody it is beneficial for them to be a little apprehensive about all that is going on around them. The initial stratagem should be dictated by the state of mind and attitude of the suspect when first approached.

The nervous suspect

Bearing in mind that the object of the stratagem is to ensure that the suspect is mildly stressed and a little apprehensive, there may be many suspects who are beyond this stage. Some are frankly fearful, even terrified, as to what is going to happen to them, and this is not the best state of mind for the purpose of a successful interview. In view of this, the approach to make to this suspect is . . .

The friendly approach

The suspect needs to be reassured that he is not going to be ill-treated, tricked or hurt in any way during the course of the proceedings. The object of the exercise is to reduce his stress level to one of mild apprehension. In view of this, when first arrested he should be dealt with in a firm but friendly manner, and can be spoken to about matters other than the offence whilst he is en route to the police station.

On arrival at the police station the procedures should be made as friendly and informal as possible, and the suspect should not be left for long periods alone in a cell before interview.

During the interview the questioner will make much use of reinforcements, smiling and nodding when the suspect makes a response to show the suspect that he is doing the right thing. The interview may turn into a sort of co-operative effort between the interviewer and the suspect with a view to getting him out of the fix he finds himself in.

It is this type of approach with the very nervous suspect which sometimes elicits a confession on the way to the police station – even though the interviewer may have avoided talking about the offence in hand.

The confident suspect

Of course many, indeed most, suspects are not lacking in confidence – some are downright cocky – and with this type of suspect the stratagem adopted above would almost certainly be counter productive. This category of suspect needs . . .

The masterful approach

Here the object is to increase the level of stress within the suspect so that his confidence is exchanged for mild apprehension. With this in mind the first approach is confident and formal. The suspect is firmly told he is under arrest and what for, and the arresting officer brooks no nonsense. On the way to the police station there is no conversation with the suspect on any subject, and any attempt by the subject to initiate a conversation is curtly rejected, especially if he implies that he has something to say which might be of interest to the interviewer – since this will enhance the state of mind which the interviewer wants to engender, ie that anything the suspect has to say is of only peripheral interest and can only benefit the suspect not the police.

At the police station the procedures should be as perfunctory and formal as possible, and the custody officer should assist. Of course the prisoner must be given his rights, but the interviewer should be allowed to give the impression that they are in his gift and that the suspect is being allowed them because there is no reason why the interviewer would wish to withhold them from him.

At the commencement of the interview the questioner will adopt a relatively impersonal attitude, as if he will listen to what the suspect has to say because it is his duty to do so but that really the content is of little importance, since the suspect will either be lying or else telling the interviewer what he already knows.

Once having heard the suspect tell his story the interviewer can then investigate the inconsistencies in it, indicate where he believes lie telling has taken place and then go on to show how this lie telling has disadvantages. It is not until the suspect adopts a less confident and more concessionary outlook that he is rewarded by reinforcing tactics – smiles, nods and a less rigid attitude on the part of the interviewer.

The hard man/soft man routine

No doubt the hard man/soft man routine has gained much popularity since it encapsulates both styles referred to above. The fact of the matter is that most suspects probably do come into the confident category and therefore it is inevitable that they need some form of control at the commencement of the interview. In truth there is no reason why one interviewer should not play both roles, indeed it may be preferable, but not all interviewers will be capable of exercising the necessary switch at the critical state of the interview with credibility, and so the practice has grown up for one interviewer to present the tough aspect of the interview whilst the other provides the gentler option.

Because the technique has become somewhat hackneyed it is no longer as credible as it undoubtedly used to be. For this reason, if for no other, it is as well for one dominant interviewer to attempt both roles if he possibly can. The trick of maintaining credibility is not so difficult: having been a little hard on the suspect at the beginning of the interview the questioner should present the friendly option only when a natural opportunity arises, as it certainly will. Suspects are quite used to this approach in their normal social environment – it is probably the way their parents and teachers handled them during their childhood development.

CHAPTER 9

Dealing with solicitors

SOLICITORS in the interview room are a fact of life and the truth is that inevitably they make life much more difficult for the interviewer. It would be folly to suggest that where persuasion of the suspect is necessary it is easier with a solicitor, because patently this is not the case. Nevertheless it is not the job of the solicitor to make life impossible for the interviewer, and there are one or two things which the interviewer can do to mitigate the damage the presence of a solicitor can do.

First it is necessary to understand exactly why the presence of solicitor is counter productive. It is not just because he may advise his client to say nothing!

As discussed in Chapter 2, isolation of the suspect from his peers is potentially an important factor in assisting the interviewer in influencing the decision-making processes of the suspect. Whilst most solicitors might baulk at the thought of being in the same peer group as most police suspects, nevertheless their job is to some extent to act as a friend to the suspect, and therefore the very presence of the solicitor removes the 'benefits' of isolation of the suspect.

In particular, even if the solicitor does not interrupt the flow of the interview, the suspect will look at him at critical points in the interview, and mere eye contact will be sufficient to give the suspect sufficient moral support to negate the influence of the interviewer. Of course, if the behaviour of the solicitor is such that the interviewing officer cannot properly put questions to the suspect, then the interviewer should consult with the duty superintendent (and in his absence with an officer not connected with the case and not below the rank of inspector) with a view to having the solicitor excluded from the interview.

The second problem with the presence of the solicitor is that his presence tends to interfere with the status of the police officer. The suspect need no longer look to the interviewer as the source of information, cigarettes and support. He can turn to his solicitor. The interviewer is no longer the most important man to the suspect, the solicitor is. Many solicitors (though not all) have all the qualities of the proficient interviewer – articulate, well dressed, well groomed, polite and well prepared – and can upstage the interviewer in the status stakes. If the interviewer is a bit short on some of these qualities then it is definitely no contest.

The latter problem is the major one. It can, however, be used to some extent to advantage the interviewer, although the trick is a difficult one for many police officers. If a confident interviewer can take control of the solicitor as well as the suspect, then to that extent the status of the interviewer is increased even further and the suspect is even more potentially susceptible to the interviewer's influence. Obviously this cannot be done by all interviewers to all solicitors, but it can be done by some interviewers to some solicitors.

As a cursory glance at the solicitors and clerks who pass along cell corridors daily in police stations up and down the country will tell, not all of those lawyers fit the bill of articulate, well dressed, well groomed, well mannered – not even well prepared – persuaders. Many of them do treat the police stations as if they own them, but this is at least in part the responsibility of those police officers with whom they come into contact. Whilst on police premises they are subject to the control of police officers, and providing the team involved with the prisoner (custody officers and interviewers do need to work as a team) then it is not beyond the wit of the experienced police interviewer to be patently in charge of all around him, including the solicitor.

So, ideally, the interviewer should certainly look good compared to the lawyer – no reason why he should not be better dressed than most of them, he probably gets paid more. He is probably bigger and should look physically fitter. If he has been selected to be a detective or dedicated police interviewer he should be at least as articulate as any lawyer (remember that many of them who visit police stations are not advocates, they are their clerks) and the police officer is on his own ground. He should use that to his own advantage.

The interviewer should introduce the lawyer to the client, and wherever possible should behave in such a way that it is clearly conveyed that not only is he in charge of the proceedings, but that he has a far better knowledge of the case than the lawyer has (which should reflect the situation as it is).

Finally, when the interview resumes with the lawyer present, the police officer should select the seating positions. The solicitor should be positioned in such a way that there can be no natural eye contact between him and the suspect, nor should he be in a position where he can easily catch the eye of the main interviewer. This makes it much more difficult for him to support the suspect non-verbally and, because he cannot have eye contact with the main interviewer, it is more difficult for him to interject and interrupt the interview verbally.

Try it out in your next interview. If not, just see how difficult it is to interrupt a conversation between two people who will not look at you and give you an easy entry.

CHAPTER 10

Preparing for the interview

WHEN asked to describe the essentials of a good interview, 46 per cent of detectives replied that it is essential for the interrogator to be well prepared. This compares with 30 per cent who said the interviewer must be calm, confident and in control, 27 per cent who said that the interviewer must possess certain special personal qualities, and approximately 20 per cent who said that the interviewer should be expert in certain ways (Walkley, 1983).

There is a great deal an interviewer can do to prepare for the interview, and it is probably one of the areas where interviewers most commonly fail.

Preparation of self

It is not sufficient to know the ingredients which go to make up the effective persuader. It is necessary for the interviewer to take positive steps to ensure that he encompasses as many of these as are possible and appropriate for the interview in hand. Many of the specific preparations (eg knowing the offence, the law, the suspect, etc) are referred to below, but there are even more basic preparations which the interviewer should make.

Those movie buffs familiar with 'The Hustler' will recall the famous battle at the pool table when Fast Eddie was finally defeated by a Minnesota Fats who, during a lull in the proceedings, took the trouble to prepare himself by washing, dressing and generally refreshing himself. In the interview room the same kind of attention to detail pays dividends.

The interviewer should attempt to ensure that he is clean, smartly dressed, well groomed, well fed, rested and free from any disability, such as a hangover. He should be equipped with the basics of his job (pens, files, paper, etc) and should have made adequate provisions for subsequent refreshment. Obviously where the interviewer has a choice, then sensible selection of the time of the interview can help in all of the above.

The law and Codes of Practice

It seems almost too elementary to point out the importance of interviewers having a sound knowledge of the law and practice under which they operate, but experience suggests that not all interrogators are as well equipped in this area as one would like them to be.

The first essential is to be totally *au fait* with the Police and Criminal Evidence Act and its Codes of Practice (see Annex A to this volume).

For example, many interviewers complain bitterly that the writing of contemporaneous notes slows down the spontaneity of question and answer, and yet ignore the option of recording an account (during the course of the interview) which adequately and accurately summarises it.

The 'summary' method can do much to ameliorate the problems created by the recording of verbatim questions and answers and is allowed for within the Code of Practice.

Similarly, many are still not aware of the change in the rules regarding the 'voluntary' principle referred to in Chapter 5, and so are still hampering themselves with out-dated restrictions, whilst others wait for hours unnecessarily for a solicitor when the delay is patently unreasonable.

Equally important is a complete understanding of the elements required to prove the case to be brought against the suspect. The points to prove have a significant bearing on the manner in which the interview is conducted.

There are often times when a suspect may persist in his denial of being an active principal but, if subtly questioned, be prepared to admit to a set of facts which constitute a lesser or inchoate offence, eg attempt, conspiracy, counselling or procuring, handling or fraud.

Know about the offence

The interrogator should know more about the offence which is the subject of the interview than any other person, save possibly the offender. Ideally he should have interviewed the complainant, and all witnesses and should certainly have visited the scene. He should ensure he has close to hand (although not necessarily in the interview room) all the documentation in relation to the case and should be completely familiar with it. Similarly he should have ready access to all the physical exhibits, including photographs where applicable.

Know the offender

It is crucial for the interrogator to have as much information about the offender as possible, and yet it has to be said that sometimes one sees police officers who go into an interview room and who have to refer to the papers in front of them to even remember the suspect's name.

The successful interviewer goes about things much more thoroughly. Of course he speaks to the collator and to CRO with a view to establishing the basics about his suspect. He also speaks to any officer who may have interviewed the suspect previously, and tries to speak to the arresting officer if he did not arrest the suspect himself. This can be difficult if the arresting officer was on nights and the interviewing officer has just arrived at 8 am, and it is regrettably true to say that in some police stations the interviewer has had to ask the suspect to describe the circumstances surrounding his arrest.

Again it seems elementary, but it bears repeating: the arresting officer in those circumstances should be expected to leave a complete and unabridged version of the arrest, including what drew his attention to the suspect, his thoughts on the case (strengths and weaknesses), anything the suspect has said since his arrest, and a list of enquiries done in relation to the arrest, together with results. If this depth of information is not available then the arresting officer should be aroused – better still, his supervisors should be aroused. The interview cannot be properly conducted without in-depth information.

A good practice is to prepare a personal history folder on the suspect himself – something separate from the file of evidence in relation to the offence committed. All the suspect's personal details should be recorded in it, together with particulars of wife, family and associates. Any idiosyncrasies he might have (eg emotional arousal at mention of his mother, susceptibility to religious influences, pet hates and foibles, unusual personal characteristics) should be noted in the folder. If the enquiry is of some importance, and there is sufficient manpower, a specific officer (not necessarily the interviewer) may be assigned to the research for and preparation of this folder.

If the interviewing officer is the arresting officer, then he can use this to his own advantage. Of course the premises in which the suspect is found will be searched, and the interviewer should always make a note of anything he sees which he might use in interview later. The arresting officer should never leave the suspect's house without making a mental note of something about which he can speak to the suspect later – if only to indicate to the suspect that he has a deeper knowledge of him than the suspect might otherwise think. Thus, the interviewer might comment on a photograph in the living room, or about something he saw in a drawer. For example, if he saw a fancy cork-screw in a drawer, he might refer to it and say, 'I didn't think you were a wine man, Joe – never seen you with anything other than a pint of bitter in your hand'.

The object of the exercise is to give the impression of an interviewer who is highly knowledgeable about the offence and the suspect's role in it, and wherever possible to indicate to the suspect that there is not much the interviewer does not know, or at least cannot find out.

Prepare a strategy

Having researched the offence and the suspect, it is not too soon to prepare a strategy, and to share that strategy with colleagues. So, the offence may be burglary and it has been established that the suspect is a persistent and confident offender. The only hard evidence is that the suspect was seen in the vicinity of the attacked premises at the right time, and the MO looks very like his.

The strategy might entail a confident, formal arrest, full and detailed search of the premises for the stolen property (even though the suspect has a reputation for not taking his property home with him), and notes to be taken regarding anything which might be useful in interview. There is to be no talking *en route* to the police station and, on arrival, the custody officer is to be as cool as possible to the suspect, and as deferential as he can bring himself to be to the arresting officer.

One of the interviewers is to be the dominant interviewer, the other the note-taker who will not be expected to contribute to the questioning in the first phase. His job is to watch the reactions of the suspect and support the line taken by the number one interviewer.

The interview itself will commence with a firm indication that this time there is plenty of evidence against the accused, but the fact that he was seen nearby is not to be mentioned, at least until the suspect has denied being anywhere near. When the vital witness is referred to, it should be almost casually as if this is by no means the most important evidence in possession of the interviewers.

Even with the simple scenario outlined above there is much pre-arrest work to be done. The two interviewers have to get their act together and ensure that they are agreed. They must speak to the custody officer to gain his support for the strategy, and they must brief the jailer so that wherever possible he will reinforce the strategy by implying that the interviewers are particularly competent, that they are very confident, and that they are in control.

In relation to any simple requests (say for a cigarette) the jailer can say that he will have a word with Mr So-and-So (the dominant interviewer), implying that it is within his gift to grant or deny requests. He can also imply at an appropriate stage that although the interviewers are tough and thorough investigators, they are also very fair – this at the later stages of the interview.

As can be seen, there is a great deal of preparation to be done with even a simple arrest. Is it often done well at your police station?

Prepare an interview room

There is probably not much that the average interviewer can do to prepare his interview room, it is a take-it or leave-it situation. Indeed, there are still quite a number of police stations without dedicated interview rooms, never mind purpose-built ones. Nevertheless, the ideal room may be described, if only to provoke debate and possibly action on the subject. After all, many purpose-built interview rooms are now being created to cater for the demands of tape recording, so now is a good time for interviewers to specify their requirements.

Extraneous noise is a distraction which the interviewer will want to avoid – any air-conditioning system should be noiseless. Similarly, sounds from the interview room should not be audible from outside – other suspects may hear what is being said, or at least be able to identify the person being interviewed from his voice. The suspect should not be able to hear conversations which are being conducted outside the interview room – sometimes these conversations reveal strength or weaknesses in the police case which should be kept from the suspect.

Other persons in custody should not be capable of identifying their cell mates, and to this end identifiable clothing or other personal property should not be left outside the cell occupied by a suspect. If it is necessary to leave clothing adjacent to a cell, and it often is, then a plastic portable wardrobe or cover should be used to disguise the owner's identity.

The room should be of adequate size to accommodate a small table (for the note-taker) and four chairs. The interviewer should prepare the room so that the suspect and he sit without the table acting as a barrier. And just in case anyone does open the door to signal to the interviewer (and they do sometimes, don't they?) the suspect should have his back to the door so that he is distracted as little as possible. The room should be in the secure area, so there should be no need for the interviewer to be closest to the door to prevent escape.

The note-taker should be more or less out of the eye line of the suspect, but should be able to see and communicate nonverbally with the dominant interviewer. Finally, the seat for the lawyer (if present) should be out of the eye line of the suspect.

The chair for the suspect should be relatively immobile and difficult to move – the feet being covered by a non-slip material. The interviewer's chair, on the other hand, should have brass or similar studs on the bottom so that during the course of the interview the interrogator can make significant shifts in his position, relative to the suspect, without any noticeable effort or break in continuity.

There should be no telephone in the room and no clock. It is not necessary for the room to be stark, but it should be bland and free from distractions – at some time the suspect's eyes are bound to wander around the room, and there should be no respite for him in visual *divertissements*.

On the wall, again preferably out of the eye line of the suspect, there should be an unobtrusive twin-cassette tape recorder. Ideally (and as far as I know no police interview room in this country has this facility) there should be an audio/visual link to another room, so that the interview can be observed by fellow team members. This enables them to keep abreast with current developments in the interview, and enables them to follow on from the previous team members with excellent continuity. The interview may also be monitored by supervisors who can advise on technique and strategy where appropriate.

CHAPTER 11

The hard men of the interview room

'DEMAND me nothing: what you know, you know; from this time forth I never will speak a word' – OTHELLO

Judging by their responses in Walkley's survey (1983), many police interviewers will be very familiar with Iago's words, having heard them uttered by what might be termed the hard men of the interview room – those who just will not respond to the interviewer's blandishments and, what's more, never look like responding.

All suspects have the right to remain silent and yet, as Irving and Hilgendorf (1980) and Softley (1980) observed in their studies, prior to the Police and Criminal Evidence Act very few did. In an observational study of 60 interviews at Lincoln police station (Walkley, 1983), only one person was observed who made a determined effort to say nothing (apart from 'No comment') but this ploy quickly crumbled in the face of a proficient police interviewer. It has to be acknowledged that the Police and Criminal Evidence Act has probably increased the likelihood of suspects saying nothing, but even now most suspects do at least converse with their interviewers.

It is no secret amongst police and criminals alike that if you are guilty of a crime it is best to say nothing in interview. It seems, however, that silence is difficult to maintain in the face of skilful and persistent interviewing, and the longer a suspect is in custody the more difficult it becomes.

In most parts of the United Kingdom there is an effective

36-hour limit on the time which a suspect may be kept in custody before being taken before a court or released from the police station, and in some areas local policy dictates a much shorter time, depending on the gravity of the case.

There is, however, a two- to seven-day limit for prisoners suspected of certain terrorist offences, and Royal Ulster Constabulary interviewers consider this longer time is an important factor in the obtaining of confessions. One Royal Ulster Constabulary detective described a successful interview:

> 'An informant told me who had committed an attempted murder; it was a terrorist attack. The informant convinced me but that was not enough. I had to convince my team that the information was good and that the suspect really had committed the crime. It was vital to convince them and I did, but after two days three of them gave up. I could tell it had become a formality for them. However, me and my partner carried on to the bitter end and eventually we won.
>
> 'I said to the suspect, "What made you cough?" He said he was sick of listening to me going on. He knew I knew, etc.
>
> 'He also said that if he'd had a cigarette on the morning of the day he broke (the third day) he thought he would have been able to hold out.'

If the attempted murder described in the preceding paragraphs had not been connected with terrorism, and there had been the same paucity of evidence, then it would have remained undetected since the police would have been barred from interviewing the suspect for the three days referred to. An inevitable consequence of the restrictions placed by the Police and Criminal Evidence Act will be that suspects for the graver crimes who had previously confessed after lengthy interviews will be less likely to confess in the future. Whilst these cases may not be great in number, they are likely to be important since they will relate to serious cases of violence and murder which will undoubtedly be repeated at some time after the suspects have been released.

The persuasive techniques described in this volume have been acknowledged by numerous detectives as being effective in interviews with 'run-of-the-mill' suspects, the bread-and-butter burglars, thieves and misfits that police officers deal with every day of the week. But in discussions with police officers from all over the country, a subject which frequently crops up is the hard man of the interview room whom no one can seem to crack – at least not within the constraints imposed on police interviewers at the present time.

What are the special qualities of the difficult subject? From the answers given in the survey it seems likely that a major problem is that he prevents the interviewer from establishing any kind of rapport with him by generating a 'hate barrier'.

During the interviews with the 100 detectives, the subjects were invited to recall a particular occasion when they had succeeded in persuading a suspect to admit an offence when an earlier interviewer had failed. Forty-two per cent of the sample said that a contributory factor in the failure of the earlier interview was that the previous interviewer had failed to establish a rapport with the suspect; that the suspect just did not like the previous interviewer.

Failure to establish a rapport can be an important contributory factor in unsuccessful interviews, but it is clear that establishing such a rapport can be difficult if the suspect is openly hostile. A significant feature of the responses on the difficult suspect was the number of occasions on which the difficult suspect was described as having a complete and utter hatred of the police.

The detectives surveyed were invited to recall a specific interview where they had failed to persuade a suspect to admit an offence, even though they (the interviewers) were convinced of his responsibility for that offence. The descriptions of the offenders by the interviewers were graphic:

> 'He's a very hard criminal. He hates me personally, I've been after him so long. He and three others committed a

> £23,000 burglary and one of the wives shopped them, but he's a really good-class criminal and he knew we couldn't have found any of the gear and he knew there were no witnesses. Even if I'd got voluntaries from the others and showed him them (which I didn't) he wouldn't have coughed. He never, ever, ever coughs. He never even says a single word, not even his name.
>
> 'He's very smart, fit, loves himself, trains regularly. When he's outside he's all mouth, slags you in the pub in front of everybody.'

The above was from a very fit, strong, experienced regional Crime Squad officer.

> 'It was a burglary in a store and he'd been caught in possession of the gear. He sat and looked at me and wouldn't even give his name. He's every detective's nightmare. He's just one of those where you've got to prove it. You've got to prove it the hard way.
>
> 'He's a bastard. He's not what I'd call a good-class criminal, because he gets caught, but he will not talk. He's the sort of bloke I admire: a big lad, can look after himself, he knows what the form is. He thinks all coppers are bastards. If you walk into a pub he's there, giving it that (*graphic gesture to indicate verbal aggression*). He's a fit lad, there's no doubt about that.'

It seems likely that this perceived implacable hatred of the police, personified in the interviewer, interferes with the rapport which interviewers feel it is necessary to develop with the suspect if he is to be successfully interviewed.

A second recognisable feature of the difficult suspect in the eyes of the police is that he is tough and physically fit. In both the examples referred to above fitness was mentioned, and it was a constant theme throughout:

> 'He's a first class, top-ten villain. He stole metal value £20,000 and an accomplice shopped him. He just sat and didn't speak, would not open his mouth. He wouldn't even say yes or no to a cup of tea.

> 'He's unbelievably evil. He's told another man to stop dealing in scrap cars otherwise he'll knee-cap him. The other chap has stopped doing the business.
>
> 'He's as awkward as he possibly can be. Won't even have a Section 1 committal. He has a complete and utter hatred of the police; heavily tattooed, 6′1″, slim, very fit.
>
> 'I think a lot of policemen are frightened of him, that's the reason he gets away with so much.'

Fitness is also mentioned in the following example:

> 'He was a little Irish man, a keep-fit fanatic. I think he was an ex-para. He wouldn't live in houses, he lived in a tent along a canal bank and was always going for training runs.
>
> 'He was in for robbing old ladies. He was little, only 5′5″ and very hairy. You can tell what he was like: one of the old ladies thought it was a hairy dog who'd jumped on her and was attacking her.
>
> 'When he was locked up he thought the bloke in the next cell had grassed him up (although he hadn't). It was at the time of the prison officers' strike and he managed to get into his cell and broke his jaw.'

It is not clear why fitness and strength should be such a valuable commodity for suspects in the interview room, but one possible answer may lie in the degree of control which interviewers feel is necessary to be brought to bear on the suspect. Thirty per cent of the sample considered that an essential ingredient of a successful interview is that the interviewer should appear to be confident and in control of the situation.

One aspect of control is undoubtedly physical, and if the interviewer loses that control because of lack of physical confidence or ability, then the interview is clearly less likely to be successful. Spurious shows of physical confidence are equally likely to be unsuccessful, even damaging. As one interviewer said in answer to a question about co-interviewers who had done something which made it harder to get a confession:

> 'My colleague threatened a suspect and there was no way he could have carried it out – the suspect would have eaten him!'

Another characteristic of the difficult suspect is his perceived lack of emotion and his apparent indifference to the consequences of his actions. For example:

> 'He'd committed loads of burglaries and t.w.o.c.'s. He's always potentially violent but totally indifferent to the feelings of others or to anything that might happen to him.'
>
> 'He just didn't care about anything. He was 6′4″ and at 24 he'd done everything, gone right through the system. Eventually he admitted a few offences out of boredom.
>
> 'After he'd been sentenced I interviewed him in prison to see if he'd write off the offences he'd committed. He wouldn't have anything to do with them. I told him we'd charge him with them. He got up, knocked me to the floor, and said "Charge me with that as well then".
>
> 'He's a target criminal, very experienced. It's against his religion to admit offences. Prison has no fear for him.'

The extracts quoted above provide a stark profile of the difficult suspect – hard, fit and uncaring. It is a profile which most experienced interviewers will have no difficulty in identifying.

As indicated at the beginning of this chapter, the writer does not purport to be able to answer the question 'How do you deal with these men?', but if the police are to increase their chances of success in the interview room with these suspects it is useful to identify their characteristics and to attempt to analyse why they present such a problem.

An analysis of other findings in the survey of police interviewers showed that they believed that, to be successful in the interview room, police officers need to:

(i) Ensure that the suspect is subject to a mild degree of stress during the interview.

(ii) Establish a rapport with the suspect.

(iii) Maintain control over him.
(iv) Influence his perception of the relative advantages and disadvantages of confession and denial.

From the description of the suspects above it is clear that it would be difficult to carry out any of these tasks in respect of them.

Routine interviews with petty criminals last about 30 minutes according to Irving and Hilgendorf (1981) in their observational study. A cursory check of the custody records in almost any police station will bear this out. However, with the difficult suspect described above, such cursory interviews are almost totally useless except as exploratory forays to prepare for the long hours yet to come. It is suggested that the length of the interview is a critical factor in most of these cases, and that supervisors and the courts must accept that in the case of the difficult suspect days rather than hours are necessary, as in the case of the interview with the terrorist suspect described earlier.

The time factor is of critical importance, since it is probably only with time that the barrier of antagonism, either real or pseudo, can be overcome and some kind of rapport established with the suspect. Once done, then the usual procedures of:

(a) Showing that denial is pointless,
(b) Indicating that denial is not cost free,
(c) Describing the advantages,
(d) Mitigating the consequences of confession,

can be adopted.

The luxury of spending a long time with the suspect may well never be available in respect of most crimes committed in this country and it is difficult to find a substitute for time. However, bearing in mind that two of the main objects of having the extra time are to overcome antagonism and establish a rapport with the suspect, it is interesting to speculate as to the type of interviewer who might be best able to accomplish this task.

Remembering that many of these difficult suspects are described as being very fit with a 'macho' image, who intimidate some male interviewers and arouse competitive or combative instincts in others, it may be that if there were available a team of well trained, skilled and experienced women interviewers they would be able to overcome the 'time' barrier.

Almost two years ago I invited any reader of *Police Review* who knew of such a team to contact me; so far the request has gone unanswered. This should not be a surprise – of the 100 detectives who were asked to describe the best interviewer they have ever worked with only one referred to a woman. It is difficult to say whether this is because so few women in the police force are good interviewers, or because most male detectives do not rate them as good interviewers – probably the latter is nearer the truth.

In spite of the lack of response it is still suggested that women interviewers might be more successful with this particular type of suspect – with the caveat that they must also have all the other qualities of the good interviewer, including intelligence and verbal fluency.

CHAPTER 12

Conclusion

IN CONCLUSION let us describe a model interview containing many of the points we have covered during the course of this book.

The interviewer will visit the scene of the crime, interview the complainant and read any statements from witnesses. He will gather together any physical evidence and examine it for himself. He will speak to the collator about his suspect, contact CRO and speak to any other officer whom he knows has interviewed the suspect in the past. He, or a colleague, will build up a dossier on the suspect to take into the interview room. The dossier will contain personal details on the suspect, together with any idiosyncrasies he might have, and information about his family, friends and associates.

He will discuss with his fellow interviewer a strategy, depending on the type of offence and the personality of the suspect, and will liaise with the jailer and custody officer, keeping them informed of his plan of campaign and enlisting their support and active participation.

During the arrest and search of the suspect's premises the interviewer will, of course, note any details which may help in the investigation of the crime, but he will also remember other things he sees so that he can later use them in interview to better understand the suspect and to foster the impression that he has a complete and intimate knowledge of the suspect and the offence.

On the way to the police station the strategy will be implemented, by either being deliberately chatty or by refraining from any communication, depending on whether the suspect needs relaxing or stressing.

At the police station the strategy is continued with the aid of the custody officer and his staff and, in particular, the custody officer does all he can to raise the status of the interviewer in the eyes of the suspect.

The suspect is taken to the interview room, where he is seated on the same side of the table as the dominant interviewer, preferably with his back to the door. At this stage the suspect is probably trying to control his body language: folded arms and legs, much eye contact, etc.

During this early stage the questions will be designed to get the suspect into 'Yes' mode. Wherever possible they will be posed in such a way that the suspect will be able to agree, and so far as is possible will be bland and unthreatening.

As the interview progresses the interviewer will be assessing the suspect's level of stress, seeking to establish the norm for the situation, and having done this will look for additional symptoms of stress at times of critical questions. If he sees these signs in response to critical questions, then this, coupled with evidence, will support the view that the suspect is telling lies. Having satisfied himself as far as he is able that the suspect is lie telling, the interview can continue with the persuasive ploys described earlier.

The interviewer will first deal with the lie-telling denials which the suspect is making and convince him that they have little or no value to him, possibly even may have certain penalties. He will hint that confession on the other hand has certain advantages. Whenever the suspect takes a step away from lie telling, he will be rewarded by suitable reinforcement ploys.

If the tactics are successful, the suspect will eventually begin to exhibit buy signs. When these signs are exhibited it is vital for the interviewer to find out (if he has not already done so) just what it is that the suspect is afraid of – what are the perceived negative consequences of confession – and, having established what these negative consequences are, should set to work on minimising them.

Once the admission comes, the suspect should be rewarded and made to feel that he has made the right decision. This is the time of potential catharsis, and if handled sensitively many suspects can be made to have a complete (or almost complete) purge of their criminal activity. If the interviewer is successful in this, then he has done an important job for society and, in many cases, has performed an equally valuable service for the suspect.

If the interviewer manages to successfully serve society and the suspect then he has achieved his objective.

ANNEX A

Extracts from the Codes of Practice to the Police and Criminal Evidence Act 1984* relating to interviews with suspects

10: Cautions

(a) When a caution must be given

10.1 A person whom there are grounds to suspect of an offence must be cautioned before any questions about it (or further questions if it is his answers to previous questions that provide grounds for suspicion) are put to him for the purpose of obtaining evidence which may be given to a court in a prosecution. He therefore need not be cautioned if questions are put for other purposes, for example, to establish his identity, his ownership of, or responsibility for, any vehicle, or the need to search him in the exercise of powers of stop and search.

10.2 When a person who is not under arrest is initially cautioned before or during an interview at a police station or other premises he must at the same time be told that he is not under arrest, is not obliged to remain with the officer but that if he does, may obtain legal advice if he wishes.

10.3 A person must be cautioned upon arrest for an offence unless:

(a) it is impracticable to do so by reason of his condition or behaviour at the time; or

(b) he has already been cautioned immediately prior to arrest in accordance with paragraph 10.1 above.

(b) Action: general

10.4 The caution shall be in the following terms:

'You do not have to say anything unless you wish to do so, but what you say may be given in evidence.'

Minor deviations do not constitute a breach of this requirement provided that the sense of the caution is preserved.

10.5 When there is a break in questioning under caution the interviewing officer must ensure that the person being questioned is aware that he remains under caution. If there is any doubt the caution should be given again in full when the interview resumes.

(c) Documentation
10.6 A record shall be made when a caution is given under this section, either in the officer's pocket book or in the interview record as appropriate.

Notes for guidance
10A – In considering whether or not to caution again after a break, the officer should bear in mind that he may have to satisfy a court that the person understood that he was still under caution when the interview resumed.
10B – It is not necessary to give or repeat a caution when informing a person who is not under arrest that he may be prosecuted for an offence.
10C – If it appears that a person does not understand what the caution means, the officer who has given it should go on to explain it in his own words.
10D – In case anyone who is given a caution is unclear about its significance, the officer concerned should explain that the caution is given in pursuance of the general principle of English law that a person need not answer any questions or provide any information which might tend to incriminate him, and that no adverse inferences from this silence may be drawn at any trial that takes place. The person should not, however, be left with a false impression that non co-operation will have no effect on his immediate treatment as, for example, his refusal to provide his name and address when charged with an offence may render him liable to detention.

11: Interview – general

(a) Action
11.1 No police officer may try to obtain answers to questions or to elicit a statement by the use of oppression, or shall indicate, except in answer to a direct question, what action will be taken on the part of the police if the person being interviewed answers questions, makes a statement or refuses to do either. If the person asks the officer directly what action will be taken in the event of his answering questions, making a statement or refusing to do either, then the officer may inform the person what action the police propose to take in that event provided that that action is itself proper and warranted.
11.2 As soon as a police officer who is making enquiries of any person about an offence believes that a prosecution should be brought against him and that there is sufficient evidence for it to succeed, he shall without delay cease to question him.

(b) Interview records
11.3 (a) An accurate record must be made of each interview with a person suspected of an offence whether or not the interview takes place at a police station.

(b) If the interview takes place in the police station or other premises:

(i) the record must state the place of the interview, the time it begins and ends, the time the record is made (if different), any breaks in the interview and the names of all those present; and must be

made on forms provided for this purpose or in the officer's pocket book or in accordance with the code of practice for the tape recording of police interviews with suspects;
(ii) the records must be made during the course of the interview, unless in the investigating officer's view this would not be practicable or would interfere with the conduct of the interview, and must constitute either a verbatim record of what has been said or, failing this, an account of the interview which adequately and accurately summarises it.

11.4 If an interview record is not made during the course of the interview it must be made as soon as practicable after its completion.
11.5 Written interview records must be timed and signed by the maker.
11.6 If an interview record is not completed in the course of the interview the reason must be recorded in the officer's pocket book.
11.7 Any refusal by a person to sign an interview record when asked to do so in accordance with the provisions of the code must itself be recorded.

12: Interview in police stations

(a) Action

12.1 If a police officer wishes to interview, or conduct enquiries which require the presence of, a detained person the custody officer is responsible for deciding whether to deliver him into his custody.
12.2 In any period of 24 hours a detained person must be allowed a continuous period of at least 8 hours for rest, free from questioning, travel or any interruption arising out of the investigation concerned. This period should normally be at night. The period of rest may not be interrupted or delayed unless there are reasonable grounds for believing that it would:

(i) involve a risk of harm to persons or serious loss of, or damage to, property;
(ii) delay unnecessarily the person's release from custody; or
(iii) otherwise prejudice the outcome of the investigation.

If a person is arrested at a police station after going there voluntarily the period of 24 hours runs from the time of arrival at the police station and not the time of his arrest.
12.3 A detained person may not be supplied with intoxicating liquor except on medical directions. No person who is unfit through drink or drugs to the extent that he is unable to appreciate the significance of questions put to him and his answers may be questioned about an alleged offence in that condition except in accordance with Annex C.
12.4 Before the commencement of an interview each interviewing officer shall identify himself and any other officers present by name and rank to the person being interviewed.
12.7 Breaks from interviewing shall be made at recognised meal times. Short breaks for refreshment shall also be provided at intervals of approximately two hours, subject to the interviewing officer's discretion to delay a break if

there are reasonable grounds for believing that it would:

(i) involve a risk of harm to persons or serious loss of, or damage to, property;

(ii) delay unnecessarily the person's release from custody; or

(iii) otherwise prejudice the outcome of the investigation.

12.8 If in the course of the interview a complaint is made by the person being questioned or on his behalf, concerning the provisions of this code then the interviewing officer shall:

(i) record it in the interview record; and

(ii) inform the custody officer, who is then responsible for dealing with it in accordance with section 9 of this code.

(b) Documentation

12.9 A record must be made of the times at which a detained person is not in the custody of the custody officer, and why; and of the reason for any refusal to deliver him out of that custody.

12.10 A record must be made of any intoxicating liquor supplied to the detained person, in accordance with paragraph 12.3 above.

12.11 Any decision to delay a break in an interview must be recorded, with grounds in the interview record.

12.12 Where the person interviewed is in the police station at the time that a written record of the interview is made, he shall be given the opportunity to read it and to sign it as correct or to indicate the respects in which he considers it inaccurate, but no person shall be kept in custody for this sole purpose. If the interview is tape recorded the arrangements set out in the relevant code of practice apply. [See *Note 12B*]

12.13 All written statements made at police stations under caution shall be written on the forms provided for the purpose.

12.14 All written statements made under caution shall be taken in accordance with Annex D to this code.

12.15 Where the appropriate adult or another third party is present at an interview and is still in the police station at the time that a written record of the interview is made, he shall be asked to read it (or any written statement taken down by a police officer) and sign it as correct or to indicate the respects in which he considers it inaccurate. If the person refuses to read or sign the record as accurate or to indicate the respects in which he considers it inaccurate, the senior officer present shall record on the record itself, in the presence of the person concerned, what has happened. If the interview is tape recorded the arrangements set out in the relevant code of practice apply.

Notes for guidance

12A – The purpose for any interview is to obtain from the person concerned his explanation of the facts, and not necessarily to obtain an admission.

12B – If the interview has been contemporaneously recorded and the record signed by the person interviewed in accordance with paragraph 12.12 above, or has been tape recorded, it is normally unnecessary to ask for a written state-

ment. Statements under caution should normally be taken in these circumstances only at the person's express wish. An officer may, however, ask him whether or not he wants to make such a statement.

12C – The police surgeon can give advice about whether or not a person is fit to be interviewed in accordance with paragraph 12.3 above.

13: Persons at risk: juveniles, and those who are mentally ill or mentally handicapped

13.1 A juvenile or a person who is mentally ill or mentally handicapped, whether suspected or not, must not be interviewed or asked to provide or sign a written statement in the absence of the appropriate adult unless Annex C applies. If he is cautioned in accordance with section 10 above in the absence of the appropriate adult, the caution must be repeated in the adult's presence (unless the interview has by then already finished).

13.2 If, having been informed of the right to legal advice under paragraph 3.6 above, the appropriate adult considers that legal advice should be taken, then the provisions of section 6 of this code apply.

13.3 Juveniles may only be interviewed at their places of education in exceptional circumstances and then only where the principal or his nominee agrees and is present.

Notes for guidance

13A – Where the parents or guardians of a person at risk are themselves suspected of involvement in the offence concerned, or are the victims of it, it may be desirable for the appropriate adult to be some other person.

13B – It is important to bear in mind that, although juveniles or persons who are mentally ill or mentally handicapped are often capable of providing reliable evidence, they may, without knowing or wishing to do so, be particularly prone in certain circumstances to provide information which is unreliable, misleading or self incriminating. Special care should therefore always be exercised in questioning such a person, and the appropriate adult involved, if there is any doubt about a person's age, mental state or capacity. Because of the risk of unreliable evidence it is also important to obtain corroboration of any facts admitted whenever possible.

13C – The appropriate adult should be informed that he is not expected to act simply as an observer. The purposes of his presence are, first, to advise the person being questioned and to observe whether or not the interview is being conducted properly and fairly; and, secondly, to facilitate communication with the person being interviewed.

13D – A juvenile should not be arrested at his place of education unless this is unavoidable. In this case the principal or his nominee must be informed.

14: Interpreters

(a) Foreign languages

14.1 Unless Annex C applies, a person must not be interviewed in the absence of a person capable of acting as interpreter if:

(a) he has difficulty in understanding English;

(b) the interviewing officer cannot himself speak the person's own language; and

(c) the person wishes an interpreter to be present.

14.2 The interviewing officer shall ensure that the interpreter makes a note of the interview at the time in the language of the person interviewed for use in the event of his being called to give evidence, and certifies its accuracy. The person shall be given an opportunity to read it or have it read to him and sign it as correct or to indicate the respects in which he considers it inaccurate. If the interview is tape recorded the arrangements set out in the relevant code of practice apply.

14.3 In the case of a person making a statement in a language other than English:

(a) the interpreter shall take down the statement in the language in which it is made;

(b) the person making the statement shall be invited to sign it; and

(c) an official English translation shall be made in due course.

(b) The deaf

14.4 If a person is deaf or there is doubt about his hearing ability, he must not be interviewed in the absence of an interpreter unless he agrees in writing to be interviewed without one or Annex C applies. [Information on obtaining the services of a suitably qualified interpreter can be found in the Codes of Practice, *Note for guidance 3C*.]

14.5 The interviewing officer shall ensure that the interpreter makes a note of the interview at the time for use in the event of his being called to give evidence and certifies its accuracy. The person shall be given an opportunity to read it and sign it as correct or to indicate the respects in which he considers it inaccurate.

(c) Additional rules for detained persons

14.6 All reasonable attempts should be made to make it clear to the detained person that interpreters will be provided at public expense.

14.7 Where paragraph 6.1 applies and the person cannot communicate with the solicitor, whether because of language or hearing difficulties, an interpreter must be called. The interpreter may not be a police officer when interpretation is needed for the purposes of obtaining legal advice. In all other cases a police officer may only interpret if he first obtains the detained person's (or the appropriate adult's) agreement in writing or if the interview is tape recorded in accordance with the relevant code of practice.

14.8 When a person who has difficulty in understanding English is charged with an offence, and the custody officer cannot himself speak the person's language, arrangements must also be made for an interpreter to explain as soon as practicable the offence concerned and any other information given by the custody officer.

(d) Documentation

14.9 Action to call an interpreter under this section and any agreement to be interviewed in the absence of an interpreter must be recorded.

Note for guidance

14A – If the interpreter is needed as a prosecution witness at the person's trial, a second interpreter must act as the court interpreter.

15: Questioning: special restrictions

15.1 If a person has been arrested by one police force on behalf of another and the lawful period of detention in respect of that offence has not yet commenced in accordance with section 41 of the Police and Criminal Evidence Act 1984 no questions may be put to him about the offence while he is in transit between forces except in order to clarify any voluntary statement made by him.

15.2 If a person is in police detention at a hospital he may not be questioned without the agreement of a responsible doctor. [See *Note 15A*]

Note for guidance

15A – If questioning takes place at a hospital under paragraph 15.2 (or on the way to or from a hospital) the period concerned counts towards the total period of detention permitted.

ANNEX B

Delay in notifying arrest or allowing access to legal advice

(A) Persons detained under the Police and Criminal Evidence Act 1984

(a) Action

1 The rights set out in 5 or 6 of the code (or both) may be delayed if the person is in police detention in connection with a serious arrestable offence, has not yet been charged with an offence and an officer of the rank of superintendent or above has reasonable grounds for believing that the exercise of each right:

- (i) will lead to interference with or harm to evidence connected with a serious arrestable offence or interference with or physical harm to other persons;
- (ii) will lead to the alerting of other persons suspected of having committed such an offence but not yet arrested for it; or

(iii) will hinder the recovery of property obtained in consequence of the commission of such an offence.

2 Access to a solicitor may not be delayed on the grounds that he might advise the person not to answer any questions or that the solicitor was initially asked to attend the police station by someone else, provided that the person himself then wishes to see the solicitor.

3 These rights may be delayed only for as long as is necessary and, subject to paragraph 6 below [regarding Persons detained under the Prevention of Terrorism (*Temporary Provisions) Act 1984*] in no case beyond 36 hours after the relevant time as defined in section 41 of the Police and Criminal Evidence Act 1984. If the above grounds cease to apply within this time, the person must as soon as practicable be asked if he wishes to exercise either right and action must be taken in accordance with the relevant section of the code.

4 A detained person must be permitted to consult a solicitor for a reasonable time before any court hearing.

(b) Documentation

5 The grounds for action under this Annex shall be recorded and the person informed of them as soon as practicable.

[Section (B) of Annex B relates to special provisions for persons detained under the Prevention of Terrorism (Temporary Provisions) Act 1984]

ANNEX C

Urgent interviews

1 If, and only if, an officer of the rank of superintendent or above considers that delay will involve an immediate risk of harm to persons or serious loss of or serious damage to property:

(a) a person heavily under the influence of drink or drugs may be interviewed in that state; or

(b) an arrested juvenile or person who is mentally ill or mentally handicapped may be interviewed in the absence of the appropriate adult; or

(c) a person who has difficulty in understanding English or who has a hearing disability may be interviewed in the absence of an interpreter.

2 Questioning under these circumstances may not continue once sufficient information to avert the immediate risk has been obtained.

3 A record shall be made of the grounds for any decision to interview a person under paragraph 1 above.

Annex C

Note for guidance

C1 – The special groups referred to in Annex C are all particularly vulnerable. The provisions of the Annex, which override safeguards designed to protect them and to minimise the risk of interviews producing unreliable evidence, should be applied only in exceptional cases of need.

BIBLIOGRAPHY

Author	Publication
Ackroyd, Carol *et al*	*Technology of political control*, Pluto Press, 1980.
Atkinson, H	*Psychology in interrogation: an evaluation of psychological research & its application to the interrogation of unwilling subjects*, Student's Paper, the Library, Police Staff College, Bramshill, Hants.
Aubry, A S & Caputo, R R	*Criminal Interrogation*, Springfield, Illinois, Charles C. Thomas, 1980.
Bennett, H G	*Committee of Inquiry into Police Interrogation Procedure in Northern Ireland*, HMSO 1979.
Bennussi, V	*Die Atmung Symptome in der Luge*, Arch. f. d. ges. Psychol., 1914, pp 244–273.
Bevan, Vaughan & Ken Lidstone	*Guide to the Police and Criminal Evidence Act 1984*, Butterworths, 1985.
Buckwalter, Art	*Interviews and Interrogations*, Woburn, Ma., Butterworths.
Calcutt, David	*Report on his enquiry into the investigations carried out by the service police in Cyprus in February and March 1984*, HMSO, 1986.
Crowley, W D	Interrogation of suspects, *International Criminal Police Review*, Aug 1973, pp 203–210.
Cunningham, C	Interrogation (address to The Medico-Legal Society) *Medico-Legal Journal*, Vol 41/2. 1973, pp 49–62.

Author	**Publication**
Cunningham, Cyril	*International interrogation techniques*, paper available at the library of the Police Staff College, Bramshill, Hants.
Ditchfield, John	Police questioning of suspects: a pilot study, *Police Review*, 9 Feb 1979, pp 208–209.
Ekman, P & Friesen, W V	Detecting deception from body and face. *Journal of Personality & Social Psychology*, 29, pp 288–298.
Firth, Alan	Interrogation, *Police Review*, 28 Nov 1975, p 1507.
Fisher, H	*Report of an enquiry into the circumstances leading to the trial of three persons on charges arising out of the death of Maxwell Confait and the fire at 27 Doggett Road, London SE6*, HMSO, 1977.
Fraser, Walter I R	Police in the judicial process: James Smart Lecture, 28 June 1972, *Police Journal*, Oct/Dec 1972, pp 262–278.
Freeman, Michael	*Police and Criminal Evidence Act, 1984*, Sweet & Maxwell, part 5.
Goodsall, J E	Professional interviewer, *Police Review*, 26 April 1974, p 525.
Goffman, E	*The presentation of self in everyday life*, Doubleday, 1959.
Gray, J	*The psychology of fear and stress*, Weidenfeld and Nicholson, 1971.
Grisso, J T & Pomieter, C	Interrogation of juveniles: an empirical study of procedures, safeguards and rights waiver, *Law & Human Behaviour*, Vol 1, No 4, 1977, pp 321–342.
Gudjonsson, Gisli	Electrodermal responsivity to interrogation and its relation to self reported emotional disturbances, *Biological Psychology*, 14 (1982), pp 213–218.
Hanson, C B	Modern interrogation techniques, *Outpost*, Sept 1972, pp 11–14.

Author	Publication
Hargreaves, Fiona & Howard Levenson	*Practitioner's Guide to the police and Criminal Evidence Act 1984*, Legal Action Group, 1985.
Hatherill, George	*Detective Story*, Deutsch, 1971, pp 57–63.
Hatherill, George	Means of interrogation, *Hong Kong Police Magazine*, Summer 1965, pp 23–30, reproduced from the *Medico-Legal Journal* Vol 32 1964, pp 164–175.
Home Office	*Police and Criminal Evidence Act 1984 (s. 66): Codes of Practice*. HMSO 1985.
Horsman, E R	Police interrogation, *Justice of the Peace*, 13 Dec 1980, pp 734–735.
Horvath, F S	Verbal and non verbal clues to truth and deception during polygraph examinations, *Journal of Police Science & Administration*, 1, pp 138–152.
Inbau, F E & Reid, J	*Criminal Interrogations & Confessions*, Baltimore, Williams & Wilkins.
Inbau, F E, Reid, J & Buckley, J	*Criminal Interrogations and Confessions*, Baltimore, London, Williams & Wilkins, 1986.
Irving, Barrie & Hilgendorf, Linden	*Police Interrogation: The Psychological Approach* *Police Interrogation: A case study of current practice*, HMSO, 1980.
James, Leslie	Questioning suspects, *Justice of the Peace*, June 1978, pp 325–327.
Killam, Edward	Interview techniques for children, *Police Chief*, July 1977, pp 22–24.
Lambert, John L	*Police Powers & Accountability*, Croom Helm, 1986 (pp 194–205).
Larson, J A	*Lying and its detection*, University of Chicago Press, 1932.
Le Taillanter, Roger	Psychological aspects of police questioning, *International Criminal Police Review*, Aug/Sept 1978, pp 190–195.

Author	**Publication**
McBarnet, Doreen	Royal Commission and the Judges' Rules, *British Journal of Law & Society*, Summer, 1981, pp 109–116.
McConville, Michael	Confessions: The dubious fruits of police interrogation, *New Law Journal*, 30 Oct 1980, pp 993–995.
McConville, Michael	Role of interrogation in crime discovery and conviction, *British Journal of Criminology*, April 1982 pp 165–175.
McConville, Michael & Baldwin, John	Questioning police interrogation, *New Law Journal*, 15 July 1982, pp 681–682.
McKinnon, Marlene	Guide to non verbal deception indicators, *Law and Order*, Jan 1982, pp 53–58.
Marston, John	*Police powers and duties: a practical guide to the Police and Criminal Evidence Act, 1984*, Fourmat Publishing, 1985, Chapter 7.
Mehrabian, A	Non verbal betrayal of feeling, *Journal of experimental research in personality*, 1971.
Mitchell, Barry	Confessions and police interrogations of suspects, *Criminal Law Review*, Sept 1983, pp 596–604.
Morris, Pauline	*Police Interrogation: Review of the Literature*, HMSO, 1980.
O'Hara, C E	*Fundamentals of Criminal Investigation*, Springfield, Illinois, Charles C. Thomas, 1970.
Palumbo, Paul	Effective interviewing: more than a mere process of questioning, *Law and Order*, Sept 1975, pp 18, 20–23.
Parker, H L	*Report of the Committee of Privy Counsellors appointed to consider authorised procedures for the interrogation of persons suspected of terrorism*, HMSO, 1972.

Author	**Publication**
Philips, C	*Report of the Royal Commission on Criminal Procedure*, HMSO, 1981.
Powell, Greg & Magrath, Chris	Police & Criminal Evidence Act 1984, a practical guide, *Longman Professional*, 1985, Part 6.
Ravier, Paul	Formulating questions and recording replies: neutrality in questioning witnesses, suspects, etc., *International Criminal Police Review*, Aug/Sept 1979 pp 190–203.
Reid, J E & Arther	Behaviour symptoms of lie detector suspects. *Journal of Criminal Law, Criminology and Police Science*, Vol. 44, 1953.
Royal F F & Schutt, S	*The gentle art of interviewing and interrogation, A professional manual and guide*, Prentice Hall, New Jersey, 1976.
Scott, Edward & Griffiths, Glen	Suggested paradigm for detectives concerning interviewing and interrogation, *Police Chief*, Jan 1978, pp 52–58.
Smith, David J	*Police and People in London, Vol 3: A survey of police officers*, Policy Studies Institute, 1983.
Softley, Paul *et al*	*Police interrogation: an observational study in four police stations*, HMSO, 1980.
Taylor, Peter	*Beating the terrorists? Interrogation at Omagh, Gough and Castlereagh*, Penguin, 1980.
Thomas, James	Police use of trickery as an interrogation technique, *Vanderbilt Law Review*, Vol 32, 1979, pp 1167–1213.
Trovillo	A history of lie detection, *Journal of Criminal Law and Criminology*, Vol 29, pp 848–849, 1939.
Trower, P *et al*	*Social skills and mental health*, Methuen, 1978.
Tully, Brian	Special care questioning, *FBI Law Enforcement Bulletin*, Nov 1985, pp 9–15.

Author	Publication
Tully, Brian & Cahill, David	*Police interviewing of the mentally handicapped: an experimental study*, Police Foundation, 1984.
Turner, A J	Comment on some aspects of the Police and Criminal Evidence Act 1984 and the Codes of Practice, *Justice of the Peace*, 15 March 1986, pp 161–165.
Unwin, Clifford	Interrogation techniques, *Police Review*, Dec 1978, pp 1874–1877.
Walkley, John	*Police Interrogation: a study of the psychology, theory & practice of police interrogation and the implications for police training*, M.Sc. thesis, Cranfield Institute of Technology, Dept. of Social Policy, 1983 (available from the library of the Cranfield Institute, Cranfield, Beds., or the library of the Police Staff College, Bramshill, Hants.)
Walters, T C & O'Connell, M A	Guide to the Police and Criminal Evidence Act, 1984, *Financial Training Publications*, 1985, Chapters 5 & 6.
Wegg-Prosser, Chas	Police and the Law, *Longman Professional*, 1986, Chapter 9.
Wicklander, D E & Hunter, F L	The influence of auxiliary sources of information in polygraph diagnoses, *Journal of Police Science & Administratin*, Vol 3, No 4, pp 405–409, 1975.
Yeschke, Charles	Nice guys make better interviewers, *Law and Order*, August 1982, pp 67–69.
Zander, Michael	*Detention for questioning: a talk*, transcription of a talk from BBC occasional series Law & Action, transmitted 23/4/77 (available from the library of the Police Staff College, Bramshill, Hants.)
Zimbardo, Philip	Psychology of Police Confessions, *Psychology Today*, June 1967, pp 17–27.

Author	**Publication**
Zuckerman, Adrian	Right against self-incrimination: an obstacle to the supervision of interrogation, *Law Quarterly Review*, Jan 1986, pp 43–70.